early years
wishing well

GW00787656

Collected rhymes, stories, songs and information text

Toys
and games

Author
Sheila Dempsey

Compilers
Stories, rhymes and
information text compiled
by Jackie Andrews

Songs compiled by Peter Morrell

Editor
Jane Bishop

Assistant Editor
Lesley Sudlow

Series Designer
Anna Oliwa

Designer
Martin Ford

Illustrations
Angie Sage

Cover artwork
Alex Ayliffe

Acknowledgements:
Qualifications and Curriculum Authority for the use of extracts from the
QCA/DfEE document *Curriculum guidance for the foundation stage*
© 2000 Qualifications and Curriculum Authority.

**The publishers gratefully acknowledge permission to reproduce the following
copyright material:**

Barbara Ball for the use of 'The weather house' by Barbara Ball © 2002, Barbara Ball, previously unpublished; **Clive Barnwell** for the use of 'Red balloon' and 'Spinning on the end of a string' by Clive Barnwell © 2002, Clive Barnwell, both previously unpublished; **Richard Caley** for the use of 'Clickety-clack!' by Richard Caley © 2002, Richard Caley, previously unpublished; **Sue Cowling** for the use of 'Hoops' by Sue Cowling © 2002, Sue Cowling, previously unpublished; **Susan Eames** for the use of 'Dressing up', 'A musical box', 'Party games', 'Six little teddies' and 'Let's play Tig' by Susan Eames © 2002, Susan Eames, all previously unpublished; **Val Jeans-Jakobsson** for the use of 'This robot' and 'Snakes and ladders' by Val Jeans-Jakobsson © 2002, Val Jeans-Jakobsson, both previously unpublished; **Karen King** for the use of 'The toyshop' by Karen King © 2002, Karen King, previously unpublished; **Patricia Leighton** for the use of 'Blowing bubbles', 'Billy's boat' and 'Amy's first kite' by Patricia Leighton © 2002, Patricia Leighton, all previously

unpublished; **Wes Magee** for the use of 'In my toy-box I have got...', 'My paintings' and 'My dinosaurs' by Wes Magee © 2002, Wes Magee, all previously unpublished; **Tony Mitton** for the use of 'What shall I be?' by Tony Mitton © 2002, Tony Mitton, previously unpublished; **David Moses** for the use of 'Bath toys' by David Moses © 2002, David Moses, previously unpublished; **Judith Nicholls** for the use of 'Sharing with Ali' by Judith Nicholls © 2002, Judith Nicholls, previously unpublished; **Sue Nicholls** for the use of 'Jigsaw bits!' and 'Rocking horse' by Sue Nicholls © 2002, Sue Nicholls, both previously unpublished; **Jan Pollard** for the use of 'Finding Teddy' and 'The puppet' by Jan Pollard © 2002, Jan Pollard, both previously unpublished; **Mandy Poots** for the use of 'Fishing' by Mandy Poots © 2002, Mandy Poots, previously unpublished; **Christine Purkis** for the use of 'My friend Tim' by Christine Purkis © 2002, Christine Purkis, previously unpublished; **Susan Quinn** for the use of 'Toyshop teddies' and 'Grandma's doll's

house' by Susan Quinn © 2002, Susan Quinn, both previously unpublished; **Coral Rumble** for the use of 'Brick on brick' by Coral Rumble © 2002, Coral Rumble, previously unpublished; **Sanchia Sewell** for the use of 'My little car is fun to push' and 'Beanbag song' by Sanchia Sewell © 2002, Sanchia Sewell, previously unpublished; **Geraldine Taylor** for the use of 'Everol's statue' by Geraldine Taylor © 2002, Geraldine Taylor, previously unpublished; **Celia Warren** for the use of 'Grandpa's Toys' by Celia Warren © 2002, Celia Warren, previously unpublished; **Stevie Ann Wilde** for the use of 'Our computers at school' by Stevie Ann Wilde © 2002, Stevie Ann Wilde, previously unpublished; **Brenda Williams** for the use of 'Street games' by Brenda Williams © 2002, Brenda Williams, previously unpublished.

Every effort has been made to trace copyright holders and the publishers apologize for any inadvertent omissions.

The author would like to thank Louise Ackerman and Sophie Edgar who helped with the initial planning of this book.

Text © 2002 Sheila Dempsey
© 2002 Scholastic Ltd

Designed using Adobe Pagemaker

Published by Scholastic Ltd, Villiers House,
Clarendon Avenue, Leamington Spa, Warwickshire CV32 5PR
Printed by Ebenezer Baylis & Son Ltd, Worcester
Visit our website at www.scholastic.co.uk

1234567890   2345678901

Contents

Introduction

Wishing Well: Toys and games 5

Rhymes

In my toy-box I have got... 6
My paintings 8
My dinosaurs 10
Blowing bubbles 12
Billy's boat 14
Clickety-clack! 16
Finding Teddy 18
The puppet 20
My friend Tim 22
Brick on brick 24
This robot 26
Snakes and ladders 28
Hoops 30
What shall I be? 32
Street games 34
Sharing with Ali 36

Information text

Our computers at school 50
Grandpa's toys 52
Grandma's doll's house 54
Dressing up 56
A musical box 58

Songs

Party games 60
Six little teddies 62
Let's play Tig 64
Bath toys 66
Jigsaw bits! 68
Rocking horse 70
Red balloon 72
Spinning on the end of a string 74
My little car is fun to push 76
Beanbag song 78

Stories

Everol's statue 38
Toyshop teddies 40
Fishing 42
Amy's first kite 44
The weather house 46
The toyshop 48

Contents

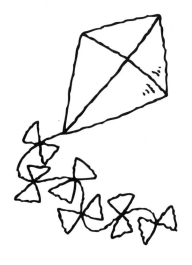

Photocopiables

Coloured glasses **80**
Different dinosaurs **81**
Blowing bubbles **82**
Let's make a boat **83**
Build a tower **84**
Design a robot **85**
Spriral snakes **86**
Moving puppet **87**
Birthday cake **88**
Teddy bear **89**
Patterned fish **90**
Colourful kites **91**
Weather symbols **92**
Jigsaw puzzle **93**
My rocking horse **94**
Make a spinner **95**
It's my body **96**

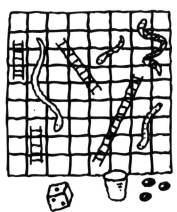

Wishing Well: Toys and games

The *Wishing Well* series is designed to help all those working with children in the Foundation Stage. The book contains a range of rhymes, stories, pieces of information text and songs with linking activities that can be used and adapted to suit children in a variety of early years settings.

Themes

'Toys and games' is a meaningful topic for all children as they will be spending much of their time engaged in play. They will have an immediate interest in talking about the toys and games that they have at home as well as a great desire to share their experiences with their friends.

Using an anthology

The activities in this book have been planned to encourage the children's imagination, their creativity and their social, as well as intellectual, development. The emphasis is on learning through play, the process being of greater importance than the product. Stories, rhymes and songs have great appeal to young children and it is important at this age to stimulate interest in all writing genre.

Most children enjoy group participation, rhyme, repetition and melody but they also have a need to question and to seek facts,

and this book will go some way to satisfying those needs.

Early Learning Goals

The ideas for using these resources are all written to support the Early Learning Goals (QCA) across the six Areas of Learning. The ideas are equally applicable to the documents on pre-school education published for Scotland, Wales and Northern Ireland.

How to use this book

The book is divided into sections, one for each type of resource, with rhymes, stories, information text and songs. Each rhyme, story, information text or song acts as a starting point for the accompanying page of activities. Photocopiable pages are also provided to support a number of the activities in the book. The resources that are recommended for the activities can be found in most early years settings or can be acquired at a reasonable cost.

Young children learn holistically and so most of the ideas in this book can be used across the curriculum and can be adapted to suit the needs and abilities of all children.

This book will help early years settings to provide activities that promote the use of imagination, develop logical thinking and extend physical and social skills as well as making learning great fun!

In my toy-box I have got...

... a blue balloon,
a quacking duck,
a plastic horse,
a sit-on truck...

... two dinosaurs,
a model farm,
a teddy bear
with just one arm...

... a ball, a bell,
old Captain Hook,
a slinky snake
and this big book...

Wes Magee

In my toy-box I have got...

Personal, social and emotional development

★ Invite the children to each bring in a special toy from home and collect the toys in a big box. During circle time, pick out one toy at a time and encourage the child who owns the toy to say why it is so special to them.

★ Talk about 'The teddy bear with just one arm' in the poem. What may have happened to him? How does he feel? What do the children do if their toys get broken? How do they feel?

Communication, language and literacy

★ As you read the poem to the children, help them to select the rhyming words. Invite them to help you devise some new verses for the poem by thinking of new rhyming words.

★ Gather resources to make your own toy box. Play 'Kim's Game', and as the children fill the box encourage them to think of new descriptive words for each toy.

Mathematical development

★ Both Captain Hook and the teddy in the poem have only one arm. Make a number story-book with the children all about the number 'one' called 'Only one' and ask the children to draw pictures of single items to illustrate it.

★ Set up a model farm with instructions for the farmer to stock the farm with one horse, two cows, three ducks and so on.

Knowledge and understanding of the world

★ Encourage the children to discover how to make wheeled vehicles move. Talk about wheels, axles and forces. Can the children discover what difference a slope makes when using these toys?

★ Discuss the different materials that the toys in the poem are made from, for example, plastic, wood, fabric and paper. Divide a large piece of paper into these four areas and ask the children to cut out pictures of toys from catalogues and magazines and stick them in the correct places.

Physical development

★ 'A quacking duck' and a 'slinky snake' are mentioned in the poem. Ask the children to think of descriptive movement sounds for other animals such as a 'mouse scurrying away from a cat' or a 'monkey swishing through the branches of the trees'. Invite them to pretend to be these animals and to practise saying some of these new descriptive words as they move.

Creative development

★ Make a collection of musical instruments. Discover the sounds that each instrument makes and then hide the instruments in a box. Make a hole in the side of the box, large enough to be able to play one instrument at a time. Ask the children to listen closely and to identify the instrument being played.

My paintings

I love to brush on reds and greens
   and watch the colours run.
I love to brush on yellow blobs.
   What is it?
      It's the sun!

I love to brush the orange on
   and lots and lots of blue.
I love to brush on purple blobs.
   Who is it?
      You! It's *you*!

Wes Magee

My paintings

Personal, social and emotional development

★ At circle time, talk about what the children love to do best. Encourage them to contribute drawings and writing and make a group book called 'I love to …'.

★ Ask the children to take a good look at each other. Do we all look the same? Encourage them to look at the differences in eye, skin and hair colour.

★ Consider how different colours can affect our moods and how we think of red for danger, and that blue is a 'cold' colour.

Communication, language and literacy

★ Create a big book using a blank big book with colour pages and ask the children to collect pictures, sort them for colour and stick them onto the correct page of the book.

★ With a small group of children experiment with some paint, watching it drip, dribble, splash and blob. Record the children's comments about how the paint reacts and make up a poem, using their ideas, to display alongside their paintings.

Mathematical development

★ Ask the children to each decide on their favourite colour. Cut out coloured 'blob' shapes for each child in the relevant colour and, during circle time, encourage each child to add their 'blob' to the group colour chart. Encourage the children to say which colour has 'more' and 'less' as well as how many 'blobs' there are.

★ Sort a bead collection and ask the children to make some repeat pattern necklaces such as red, yellow, red, yellow.

Knowledge and understanding of the world

★ Set up some 'colour tasting' sessions! On green day, for example, you might invite the children to taste kiwi, cabbage, lettuce or grapes. Ask the children to describe the tastes and to say if the colour make a difference?

★ Provide a copy of the photocopiable sheet on page 80 and ask the children to each decorate a pair of sun-glasses. Let them choose coloured Cellophane for the eye pieces and ask them to talk about how the world looks through their coloured glasses!

Physical development

★ During movement time, ask the children to pretend to be artists, dipping their brushes and painting with a flourish. Next, ask them to be the paint itself – dripping, running, blobbing and finally coming to rest to dry.

Creative development

★ Make symmetrical paintings by dropping blobs of paint on one half of a folded piece of paper, pressing together and then opening it up. Encourage the children to notice the mirror images, the mix of colours as well as the pictorial content.

My dinosaurs

I have ten model dinosaurs.
What teeth they've got... and horns... and claws!

They stand in line beside my bed.
They're coloured orange, brown or red.

The Brontosaurs have long, long necks.
I *love* Tyrannosaurus Rex!

Wes Magee

My dinosaurs

Personal, social and emotional development

★ Ask the children which toys they keep beside their beds and why they are special.

Communication, language and literacy

★ Make a collection of dinosaur books both fiction and non-fiction. Help the children to find out some facts and to make a dinosaur book with pictures and information to add to the book corner.

★ Ask the children to close their eyes and imagine what the ten dinosaurs do when the child in the poem is fast asleep. Record the children's responses and add them to the dinosaur book.

★ Hide a selection of different toy animals in a box, select one and play an 'I spy' game, using initial sounds or descriptive words, to help the children guess the chosen animal.

Mathematical development

★ Choose one toy dinosaur and ask a few children at a time to find something in the room that is smaller or bigger, longer or shorter than the dinosaur.

★ Make a collection of toy dinosaurs and ask the children to decide on a criteria for sorting them such as by size, colour or how fierce they are.

★ Make a bed for the dinosaurs and sing a new song to the tune of 'There were ten in the bed'.

Knowledge and understanding of the world

★ Tell the children that other animals have teeth, claws and horns. Find out what these are, why they have them and what they use them for. Talk about how our hair, nails and teeth grow and how we must look after them to keep ourselves healthy.

★ Find out what happened to dinosaurs. Talk about other animals that are in danger of extinction, and consider what we can do to care for our world.

Physical development

★ Chalk a large bed (square) on the playground and play a positional game, calling out instructions for the children such as 'Jump on the bed', or 'Hop beside the bed'.

★ Divide the children into teams and give each team the name of a dinosaur. Devise an obstacle course and find out which dinosaur team will win the race.

Creative development

★ Laminate some copies of the photocopiable sheet on page 81 and challenge the children to use play dough to make ten different dinosaurs.

★ Create a dinosaur model using a collection of big boxes and other junk materials, and pictures of dinosaurs as reference. Allow the children to work in small groups on this big model over a period of days, adding textures and colours to make it look as real as possible.

Early years wishing well: Toys and games

Blowing bubbles

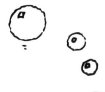

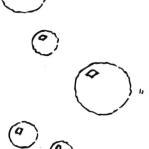

Bubbles are beautiful
Bubbles are fun
Bubbles are rainbows
Caught in the sun.

Bubbles float up
Bubbles float down
Bubbles float sideways
And round and round.

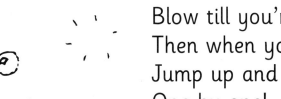

Blow till you're breathless
Then when you've done
Jump up and burst them
One by one!

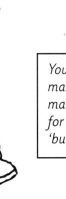

> You can use this poem as an action rhyme by making big round arm shapes for bubbles, making a rainbow, moving arms in directions for verse 2, then a big jump up and imaginary 'bursting' session at the end.

Patricia Leighton

Blowing bubbles

Personal, social and emotional development

★ Talk about what the children think of as beautiful. Make a 'beautifully' decorated list of all of the children's ideas and display this alongside a collection of 'beautiful' objects, both natural and manufactured. Invite the children to bring some of their 'beautiful' objects from home to add to the display.

★ Ask the children to talk about how they feel when precious things get broken. How do they help their friends to feel better when they are upset?

Communication, language and literacy

★ Go on a pretend journey in a bubble with the children. Sit together underneath a parachute and talk about what it feels like to be trapped inside the bubble and about what you can see outside the bubble.

★ Read *One, Two Flea!* by Allan Ahlberg and Colin McNaughton (Walker Books) to the children.

Mathematical development

★ Ask the children to make a secret tally of how many times you say the word 'bubbles' while you read the poem. Check to see how many children have counted correctly (seven) when the reading is finished.

★ Blow some bubbles and ask the children to start counting. How high can they count to before all the bubbles have burst?

Knowledge and understanding of the world

★ Experiment with blowing bubbles using different closed shapes such as straws or tubes. Are all the bubbles the same shape? Challenge the children to blow a bubble that is not round. Use wire to make square and triangular bubble loops and ask the children what shapes the bubbles will be and why.

★ Ask the children to look into some bubbles. Can they see their own reflections? Where else can they see their reflections? Have a collection of reflective objects such as mirrors and spoons for the children to explore.

★ Encourage the children to talk through their ideas of how bubbles stay up in the air and about other things that float in the air.

Physical development

★ Let the children colour the bubbles on the photocopiable sheet on page 82, then cut them out to add to a bubble display.

★ During movement time, give each child a ribbon streamer. Encourage them to run and dance with the streamers up high, down low and spinning round and round.

Creative development

★ Cut circles of paper the same size as a shallow tray. Mix paint with a little water and some washing-up liquid. Let the children use straws to blow bubbles in the mixture and then to take prints of the bubbles by carefully resting the paper on top of the mixture.

Billy's boat

(Action rhyme)

Billy had a little boat
Just this big.
His grandad made it out of wood
And gave it to him.

*(index fingers apart to show size,
hammering/sawing, 'giving' gesture)*

Its sail was cotton silver,
Its name was painted gold,
It had an anchor on the side
And toffees in the hold.

*(mime sail triangle, painting a name,
swinging finger side to side (anchor),
rubbing tummy)*

Billy sailed his little boat
Up and down the stream
Until the day was over
And walked home in a dream.

*(bobbing wave movements side to side
with hand, 'finger walking')*

He put his boat up on the shelf,
Took one last peep,
Then snuggled down into his bed
And sailed away to sleep.

*(mime putting boat on shelf, peep between
hands, left hand in gentle wave
movements until joins right hand, cheek on
both hands, close eyes)*

Patricia Leighton

Early years wishing well: Toys and games

Billy's boat

Personal, social and emotional development

★ Discuss with the children what special routines they have before going to bed. Encourage them to talk about supper, bathtime and bedtime stories.

★ In the rhyme, Billy had toffees in the hold of his boat. Ask the children what special food they would choose to take on journeys.

★ Talk together about present giving. Ask the children when they receive presents, how it makes them feel. Do they enjoy giving presents too?

Communication, language and literacy

★ Make zigzag books for the children to record, with illustrations, four different events in the rhyme, in the correct sequence.

★ Gather a collection of books both fiction and non-fiction which feature boats and sailing. If possible, bring in some real sailing resources for the children to handle.

★ Help the children to construct a role-play boat. Use large boxes or bricks to build the hold and challenge the children to make an anchor, a sail and a treasure chest. When it is complete, set sail for imaginary adventures!

Mathematical development

★ Float some plastic dishes in the water tray and ask small groups of children to count how many pebbles they can put in the trays before they sink.

Knowledge and understanding of the world

★ Challenge the children to design and make a flag for their own boat, using fabric paints or crayons on pieces of cotton sheeting.

★ Make boats with junk materials. Discover whether the boats really sail in the water tray, and, if not, encourage the children to adapt their designs and to talk about their decision-making.

Physical development

★ Talk through, and let the children act out, the drama of a sailing journey: put up the sails, scrub the decks, climb the rigging and search for buried treasure.

★ Go on a movement map journey to find the treasure. Tell the children how many paces forward, backwards and sideways they need to take before digging for their treasure.

Creative development

★ Collect blue and green fabrics to make a sculpture stream. Give each child a piece of wooden rod and encourage them to wind the fabrics around their rods. As each child completes the task, join the rods to form a ladder-like construction to hang from the ceiling. Suspend 'watery' words nearby.

★ Encourage the children to paint a stream using watery paint. Then use the photocopiable sheet on page 83 for the children to cut and stick their own boats to sail on their watery stream pictures.

Clickety-clack!

Clickety-click!
Clickety-clack!
Tommy the toy train's
Out on his track
Under the tunnel
Round the bend
Back to the station
Journey's end.

Richard Caley

Rhymes

Clickety-clack!

Personal, social and emotional development

★ Ask the children to tell you about special journeys that they have made. Encourage them to say how they travelled, where they went, who went with them and whether anybody met them at the end.

★ Explain that saying goodbye is difficult sometimes. Let the children talk about how they feel when they have to say goodbye to somebody that they love.

Communication, language and literacy

★ Build a role-play train, dress up and go on an imaginative train journey. Make a collection of timetables, tickets and brochures to encourage the children in their play.

★ Invite the children to think of other onomatopoaic words which are similar to 'clickety-clack' such as 'trippety-trap' and 'snippety-snap'.

Mathematical development

★ Make a birthday train with a carriage for each month of the year for your wall. Invite each child and member of staff to paint a picture or stick a photograph of themselves in the correct carriage.

★ Make a toy train track with a tunnel, an engine and five carriages and encourage the children to work out problems such as 'We can see the engine and two carriages, how many carriages are still in the tunnel?'.

Knowledge and understanding of the world

★ Take the children on a short train journey; ideally on a steam train.

★ Compare pictures of steam trains and present day trains. Look for similarities and differences.

★ Some of the children may have been on a journey through the Channel Tunnel. Invite them to talk about their journey to a different country.

Physical development

★ Set up an obstacle circuit for the children to explore providing opportunities for them to balance along objects, crawl through them and climb up and down.

★ Challenge some of the children to be tunnels, keeping both their feet and their hands on the floor while their friends find different ways to go through the tunnels: forwards, backwards, crawling or sliding.

Creative development

★ Let the children use musical instruments to make steady beat 'clickety-clack' sounds. Ask them to continue playing in time as you read the poem. Try working at different speeds!

★ Provide rectangles of painting paper and challenge the children to paint a picture that they might see from a train window. Cover the pictures with clear food wrapping (to represent window glass) and add a frame. Display the pictures in a line.

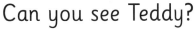

Finding Teddy

Can you see Teddy?
Is he over there?   (pointing)
Can you see Teddy?
Is he under a chair?   (looking)
Where is our teddy?
Is he up in the air?   (pointing)
Wherever is our teddy?
Who can find our bear?

> Close eyes while the children take turns to hide the bear.
> Repeat the questions.

Jan Pollard

Finding Teddy

Personal, social and emotional development

★ Ask the children to talk about how they feel if they mislay their favourite toys, and how they feel when they find them again.

★ Contact the 'Guide Dogs for the Blind Association' and invite a volunteer to come to talk to your group about their work with the visually impaired.

Communication, language and literacy

★ Help the children to recognize questions are answered by more questions in the poem. Point out that most questions begin with the words 'who', 'why', 'when', 'what', 'where' or 'how'.

★Think about different hand movements and expressions and help the children to make a collection of pictures that portray different needs and emotions.

Mathematical development

★ Hide a favourite teddy in the setting and give the children clues to help them find him. Extend this activity by using a range of positional language such as 'Look behind the curtain' or 'Have you looked on top of the cupboard?'.

★ Role-play the story of 'Goldilocks and the Three Bears' (Traditional) and encourage the children to use mathematical language such as 'biggest', 'smallest', 'middle sized', 'first', 'second' and 'third'.

Knowledge and understanding of the world

★ Invite the children to make a junk model construction in which to hide a teddy, for example, a treasure box, a house or a vehicle. Encourage them to talk about their constructions and scribe their ideas to display with their finished work.

★ Make a simple map of your setting together. Ask a helper to secretly hide a teddy and then put a mark on the map to indicate where the teddy is hidden. Can the children follow the map to find the teddy?

Physical development

★ Play 'Teddy hide-and-seek' by hiding five teddies around the setting and encouraging the children to search for them. Let the child who finds the fifth teddy, hide all the teddies in different places ready for a new search.

★ During a movement session ask the children to show you how they would change their body shapes if they wanted to hide in a box, under a blanket or behind a door.

Creative development

★ Invite the children to colour pictures of their own teddies. Cut pieces of paper large enough to cover the teddies and make hiding-place pictures for the bears. Stick the second pictures as flaps to hide the first. Display these in the setting with questions such as 'Where is Sam's bear hiding?' or 'Whose bear is hiding behind the box?'.

The puppet

Here is a puppet
on a string.
You can make him do
just anything.
Lift up his hand
to scratch his nose.
Bend him over
to touch his toes.
One foot up
and one foot down.
Here he goes,
walking into town.

Pretend you're a puppet
on a string.
And someone can make you
do anything.

Jan Pollard

Early years wishing well: Toys and games

The puppet

Personal, social and emotional development

★ Talk sympathetically to the children about times when they do not want to do what they are supposed to be doing. Suggest ways that some of these situations might be resolved.
★ Discuss sensitively times when the children should not let somebody make them do things that they do not want to do.

Communication, language and literacy

★ Play 'Croaker' where a talking puppet gets his words wrong and the children have to correct him.
★ Sing movement songs together such as 'One finger, one thumb keep moving' from *This Little Puffin...* compiled by Elizabeth Matterson (Puffin). Invite the children to join in singing and doing the accompanying hand actions, finally reciting the complete rhyme with no words at all just movements.

Mathematical development

★ Play 'Simon says one' where each instruction has to include the number one, for example, 'Simon says stand on one leg' or 'Simon says put one hand on your head'. The children miss a turn if they respond to instructions that mention other numbers, for example, 'Simon says wave two hands'.
★ Use finger puppets to sing number rhymes, encouraging the children's awareness of addition and subtraction.

Knowledge and understanding of the world

★ Read the story of 'Pinocchio' (Traditional) and talk about different types of puppet. Encourage the children to make some of their own: a simple string puppet can be made by tying strings to the arms and legs of a rag doll and then suspending it from a stick; hand puppets are easily made from socks decorated with mouths and other features.
★ Make a collection of programmable and programmed toys and explore them together.

Physical development

★ Play some lively music and challenge the children to move like puppets held up with strings. When the music stops, the children should flop to the floor and remain motionless until the music starts again.
★ During movement time, ask the children to stand face-to-face with a partner and to hold both hands with them. As one child begins to move the other moves too, just like a puppeteer controlling a puppet.

Creative development

★ Draw around one child on strong card and cut the shape into the different body parts. Decide on a character and ask the children to paint the pieces of the life-sized puppet appropriately. When the pieces are complete, reassemble the puppet with split pins and use strings to suspend the puppet from the ceiling for the children to interact with it.

My friend Tim

I've a special friend
His name is Tim
He likes me
And I like him.
He lives quite near –
Not far away –
And every day
He comes to play.
He doesn't mind
What games I choose.
I always win
He likes to lose.
He waits until
I've had my tea
And then we sit
And watch TV.
I like him
And he likes me.
Tim's invisible,
You see.

Christine Purkis

Early years wishing well: Toys and games

My friend Tim

Personal, social and emotional development

★ Invite the children to discuss their special friends in the setting. Let them draw pictures and take photographs of each other to make a 'My special friend book'.

★ Ask if any of the children have a special invisible friend. If so, ask if they have a name, and what special things they do together. Play board games such as *Snakes and Ladders* with the children and help them to understand about winning and losing.

Communication, language and literacy

★ Read the poem carefully to the children and help them to pick out the rhyming words. Ask them to add more rhyming words to each rhyming pair to make rhyme lists for example, choose, lose, shoes, snooze.

★ Challenge the children to write their own names and then the name of their best friend.

★ Use white wax crayons on white paper to write some 'invisible' messages, use a thin colour paint wash to reveal the secrets!

Mathematical development

★ Talk together about where the children's friends live. Ask them to think about what colour their front door is, what number is on the door and how many people live at their friend's houses.

★ Use photographs or other resources to help the children gain an understanding of the passage of time, putting them in order to represent a day in your setting.

Knowledge and understanding of the world

★ Talk about what the children do when they are not at the setting. What are their favourite games? Make a pictogram of the results.

★ The television needs electricity to work. Challenge the children to make lists or find pictures of other things in the home that need electricity to work.

★ Use musical instruments to explain the meaning of 'invisible' – the sound is there but you cannot touch it or see it!

Physical development

★ Play circle games such as 'The Farmer's in his Den' and 'Ring-a-Ring-o' Roses' to encourage co-operative group play.

★ Stand the children behind a line in the playground and place some hoops near to and some far from them. Encourage them to take turns to throw beanbags into the hoops.

Creative development

★ Make some play dough with the children, adding a variety of food colourings. Give the children a paper plate each and ask them to make their favourite play-dough tea.

★ Give the children a safety mirror and ask them to draw themselves. Make attractive frames for these drawings and display them with the caption 'Mirror, mirror on the wall'.

Brick on brick

Brick on brick

Building high

Tower model

To the sky

Push and snap

Brick on brick

Making walls

Strong and thick

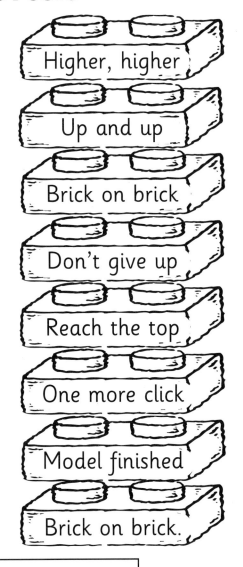

Higher, higher

Up and up

Brick on brick

Don't give up

Reach the top

One more click

Model finished

Brick on brick.

Stick the different lines on to boxes or Lego bricks. Let the children 'build' the poem line by line. They will soon discover that the poem works best when the lines are reversed, with the first line at the bottom, the second line goes on top of that and so on.

Coral Rumble

Brick on brick

Personal, social and emotional development

★ Encourage the children to work with a friend and to take turns to build each storey of a tower. If each partner chooses a different coloured set of bricks, the children will begin to notice patterns emerging from their co-operative play.

★ Talk about working together and how we can help one another to achieve a goal.

Communication, language and literacy

★ 'Rapunzel' lived high in a tower and 'Humpty Dumpty' was on top of a wall, discuss ways in which the children could rescue these fictional characters.

★ Cut some brick-shaped paper and encourage the children to draw or write about their own homes on their own 'brick'. Mount the bricks to make a group house or tower to display in the setting.

Mathematical development

★ The tower in the poem gets 'higher'. Invite a child to help you order the children in height from the shortest to the tallest, and then from the tallest to the shortest. Can the children notice a pattern in their ordering?

★ As the children build their own towers keep a metre rule to hand and help them to measure their towers. Keep a record of the children's achievement and award a 'Best builder' sticker at the end of the session.

★ Show the children a house brick and encourage them to notice the different-sized rectangles on each face of the brick. Take rubbings from each face and help the children to construct a 3-D paper brick.

Knowledge and understanding of the world

★ Look at information books and find out how real bricks are made. Take the children on a walk to look at patterns on brick walls.

★ Invite a local builder into your setting to talk to the children about how brick walls are safely constructed, and about the materials and tools required.

Physical development

★ During movement time, ask the children to imagine what it would be like to be builders. Invite them to mime putting on their hard hats and their overalls and to mix the mortar with cement, sand and water. Encourage them to build their own walls and, of course, to stand back and admire their work and that of their fellow builders!

Creative development

★ Make a big collection of different-sized boxes. Give the children plenty of space (outdoors if possible) to build towers and to watch them tumble.

★ Challenge the children to use the photocopiable sheet on page 84 to cut, design and stick their own towers.

This robot

(Action rhyme)

This robot can stand.   (stand stiffly)
This robot can talk.   (open and close mouth)
This robot can jump.   (jump on the spot)
This robot can walk.   (walk on the spot)

We made him from boxes
And packets and string,
Wire, lids and tinfoil –
All sorts of things.

He's driving a car.   (turn 'steering wheel')
He's running to school.   (run on the spot)
He's climbing the stairs.   ('climb' on the spot)
He's really so COOL!   (thumbs up)

Val Jeans-Jakobsson

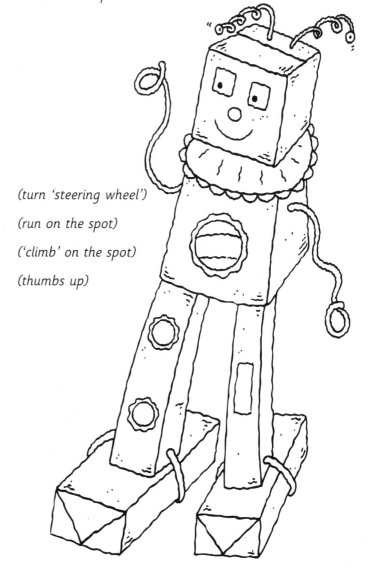

Early years wishing well: **Toys and games**

This robot

Personal, social and emotional development

★ Explain how a robot can only do things that it is commanded to do. Encourage the children to understand that they are not robots and to celebrate that they are all different and all very special.

★ Ask the children to imagine that they have a robot of their own to command. What jobs would they ask the robot to do for them?

Communication, language and literacy

★ Say the poem using a robotic voice and ask the children to try out robotic voices when answering your questions about the poem. Record your robot conversations and play them back for the children to listen to.

★ Use cardboard tubes or tissue paper and combs to make more unusual sounds with the children.

★ Make a pictorial list of all of the things the robot in the poem can do. Ask the children to think of other activities for the robot, add these to the poem with appropriate actions.

Mathematical development

★ Invite the children to cut, design and stick their own robot using the photocopiable sheet on page 85.

★ Use junk materials to make a robot with the children, encouraging them to recognize shapes and to count faces and corners of the boxes which they decide to use.

★ Pretend that your junk robot keeps making mistakes when it is counting, leaving numbers out, or muddling numbers up. Can the children recite the numbers to ten and put the numbers in the correct order?

Knowledge and understanding of the world

★ Make a collection of programmable toys and help the children to discover how these toys work.

★ Encourage the children to recognize the differences and similarities between robots and us, and to discuss the differences between living and non-living things.

Physical development

★ During a movement session, ask the children to move like robots, following instructions. How will they move, how fast will they go and what will happen if their batteries run out?

★ Play 'Can you' during outdoor play. Each time you blow the whistle, give the children a new challenge such as to hop or walk backwards.

Creative development

★ Create a workshop environment in your role-play area. Encourage the children to draw robots and make plans of how they can make a robot using the construction equipment. Be on hand to record their ideas about what their robots can do and how they work.

Snakes and ladders

Up the ladder
And down the snake,
Throw the dice –
A move to make.

Some ladders short,
Some ladders tall,
Climb right up
To the top of the wall.

But a fat little snake
Is waiting for me,
When I shake the dice
And it rolls out – three!

I reach the top
And I'm nearly there,
But a slippery snake
Is in the next square!

I shake the dice
And say, 'Make it two!'
Phew! I made it,
So I beat YOU!

Val Jeans-Jakobsson

Early years wishing well: Toys and games

Snakes and ladders

Personal, social and emotional development

★ Encourage the children to play board games to encourage taking turns and instil an understanding of winning and losing.

★ Some children have a fear of snakes. Make a collection of books, pictures and facts about snakes to endeavour to put some of these fears to rest.

Communication, language and literacy

★ Repeat the words 'slippery snake' to the children and encourage them to add more descriptive 's' words to extend the phrase. Write out the words and make an 's' word snake by adding a decorated head and tail.

★ Make some snake puppets using old socks for the bodies and buttons for the eyes. Encourage the children to use the puppets for imaginative conversations.

Mathematical development

★ Make a collection of snakes from old coloured tights – some long, some short, some fat and some thin. Give the snakes eyes and some decoration. Keep the snakes in a covered laundry basket and allow the children to pull them out, one at a time, to discuss, compare, measure and count.

★ Cut lengths of different-coloured painting paper into snake shapes and encourage the children to use two different print blocks to give their snake a repeating pattern.

Knowledge and understanding of the world

★ Make a snake book with pictures that the children have made, together with some snake facts. Find out what snakes eat and whether they lay eggs or give birth to babies.

★ Build an environment in the sand tray for a collection of plastic snakes to encourage the children to use their factual knowledge about snakes to enhance their imaginative play.

Physical development

★ Create a route for the children to follow to involve sliding on tummies and backs, and crawling on hands and knees. Make a dice with pictorial instructions on each face.

★ Suggest that the climbing frame is similar to a gameboard from *Snakes and Ladders*. Encourage the children to slither between the bars and to climb up and down the ladders.

Creative development

★ Make a 3-D 'Snakes and Ladders' display. Divide a large display board into squares and give each child a numbered square to paint. Pin the numbers to the board and then make some stuffed and decorated snakes from fabric, some ladders from cardboard tubes and a large dice from a cube-shaped box. Lay out a real game of *Snakes and Ladders* for the children to play on a table below the display.

★ Use the photocopiable sheet on page 86 to make spiral number snakes to hang from the ceiling in your setting.

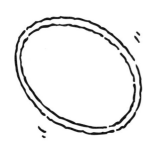

Hoops

Hoops on the ground
Jump out! Jump in!
Hoops round our waists
To twirl and spin.
Hoops in the air
To catch and throw.
Hoops in the cupboard –
Away they go!

Sue Cowling

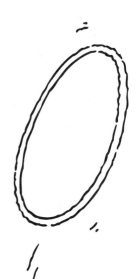

Early years wishing well: Toys and games

Hoops

Personal, social and emotional development

★ Sit the children in a circle and explain that you are going to play 'Pass the hoop, pass the face'. As the hoop is passed from one child to another, they should each make a face to their neighbour through the hoop such as a funny face, sad face, worried face or happy face.

★ Talk about what rings signify, for example, wedding rings and eternity rings.

Communication, language and literacy

★ Make a collection of words with the 'oo' sound such as moon, balloon and spoon. Display these objects and the words written on card in a hoop.

★ Go on a circle shape hunt with the children, take a camera and record your discoveries. Encourage the children to draw and write on circular paper about something round which they saw during the hunt and join these together to make a circle big book.

Mathematical development

★ Use hoops during movement time to explore positional language. Ask the children to stand *in* their hoops, *out of* their hoops, *on* their hoops and to hold their hoops *over* their heads or *behind* their backs.

★ Place a hoop in the play area, draw a line approximately two metres away and encourage the children to throw coloured beanbags into the hoop and count them.

Knowledge and understanding of the world

★ Make ring biscuits with the children. Ask them if there are any other foods which they eat that are also hoop shaped such as spaghetti hoops, doughnuts or onion rings.

★ If possible, bring a bicycle into the setting and encourage the children to look at it carefully to find as many circle shapes as they can. Investigate why wheels have to be round and challenge the children to use this knowledge to design and make their own wheeled vehicles.

Physical development

★ During movement time, let the children find out how many different ways they can hold a hoop such as on their fingers, arms and legs. Then experiment to find out what the hoop can do. Can the children make their hoops roll and spin?

★ Invite the children to play 'Foot in the hoop' by placing different-coloured hoops around the play area. Ask the children to run about. When you shout a colour, the children should place just one foot into the correct coloured hoop.

Creative development

★ Sit the children in a circle and play 'Pass the sound' or 'Pass the rhythm' using different percussion instruments. Look for circles in your collection of instruments such as in tambourines and drums.

Early years wishing well: Toys and games

What shall I be?

I can dress as a wizard.
I can dress as a knight.
I can even dress as a dragon,
Growling for a fight.

I can dress as a pilot,
Or an astronaut instead.
Or maybe a googly alien
With bleepers on my head.

I can dress as a pirate,
Digging down deep for gold.
Or a lonely, lost explorer,
Struggling through the cold.

I can dress as anyone
With a hat or a coat or a scarf.
With big, baggy pants I can dress as a clown –
There! I've made you laugh...

Tony Mitton

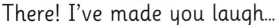

What shall I be?

Personal, social and emotional development

★ During circle time, ask the children what they would like to be when they are grown up and why. Have a collection of books about different jobs and professions available for the children to explore.

★ Ask the children if they have ever been lost like the explorer in the poem. How did they feel? What should they do if they feel lost?

Communication, language and literacy

★ Invite the children to dress up in the role-play area. Encourage their conversation between the different characters in role. Use a tape recorder to record interviews with each character asking questions such as 'What do you wear for your job?', 'Do you help other people?' and 'Do you have a dangerous job?'.

★ Explain that wizards write spells. Give the children cauldron-shaped paper and challenge them to write or draw their own spells, listing the ingredients, and the outcome!

Mathematical development

★ Provide a postman's hat, brown sack and a collection of letters and say the rhyme 'Ten Little Letters in a Brown Sack' from *This Little Puffin...* compiled by Elizabeth Matterson (Puffin).

★ Bury some 1p coins in the sand tray. Invite the children to dig for gold using scoops and sieves! Who will be first to find five coins?

Knowledge and understanding of the world

★ Make a collection of hats and during circle time, invite the children, one at a time, to choose a hat and mime the job for which the hat is worn.

★ Talk about how explorers travel all over the world. Let the children look at a globe and an atlas and find out about different countries and climates. Collect resources to help the children to gain a knowledge and understanding of different parts of the world.

Physical development

★ Make time for the children to put on and fasten their own coats at playtime or home time. Put up a list for carers to see who is succeeding with this task and encourage them to let their children practise at home.

★ Be clowns during movement time. Can the children balance along a rope on the ground? Can they juggle with two beanbags?

Creative development

★ Create a fancy dress shop in the role-play area. Encourage the children to choose a character or profession and to dress appropriately. Have a range of 'tools of the trades' available, for example, a wand for a magician or a stethoscope for a doctor, so that the children can act our their chosen role.

★ Challenge the children to decorate their own moving puppet by using the model on the photocopiable sheet on page 87 .

Street games

Tops and whips
And hopscotch
Playing with a ball.

Tallyho
Tick on high
Handstands up the wall.

Skipping games
With long rope
Running out and in.

Roller-skates
And cricket
Stumps drawn on a bin.

'I spy' games
In windows
Of shops on winter nights.

Scary ghosts
In shadows
Running back to light.

Swinging
On the lamppost
In the gaslight glow.

This is how
My grandma played
A long time ago.

Brenda Williams

Early years wishing well: Toys and games

Street games

Personal, social and emotional development

★ Talk about why grandparents are special and ask the children to tell the others some of the things they do with their grandparents.

★ Invite a grandparent or great-grandparent into the setting to tell the children about the games that they played when they were children. Have some of these old-fashioned toys or replicas for the speaker to use as resources and for the children to handle.

Communication, language and literacy

★ Teach the children some playground chants which children sang while they were playing or deciding turns such as 'One potato, two potato'.

★ Make a collection of familiar objects and place them in the centre of the circle at circle time. Play 'I spy' initially by description, for example, 'I spy something that is brown and furry' and then by initial sound, for example, 'I spy something beginning with "t"'.

Mathematical development

★ Chalk a hopscotch grid in the outdoor play area and challenge the children to hop or jump from number one to number ten and then to count and hop backward to the beginning again.

★ Play number games which children played in the children's grandparent's childhood such as dominoes or skittles.

Knowledge and understanding of the world

★ Collect some pictures of children playing in the street years ago. Compare the scene with a typically busy, present day street scene and talk about similarities and differences.

★ Explore what life without electricity and television might have been like. Explain to the children what 'in the gaslight glow' means and learn rhymes such as 'In winter I get up at night and dress by yellow candlelight, in summer quite the other way I often go to bed by day' by Robert Louis Stevenson (in *A Child's Garden of Verses*).

Physical development

★ Use a large torch or projector to make a shadow wall and show the children how to make their own 'scary ghost' body shape performances and discover more about shadows and how they are made.

★ Play with skipping ropes, bats and balls and try to recreate some of the games which children used to play years ago.

Creative development

★ Look at some paintings by Lowry where children can be seen playing the games mentioned in the poem. Ask the children to paint pictures of themselves with their friends playing their favourite games.

★ Make some spinning tops by decorating circles of card and then piercing the centre with a pencil to use as a spinning stick.

Sharing with Ali

I'll share my cars
and I'll share my paints,
I'll share my tent by the tree.
I'll share my puzzles although they're new,
I'll share my paper, I'll share my glue...
but *please* don't ask for my pirate ship;
that is just for me.

I'll share my scooter,
and even my bike,
and buckets and spades by the sea.
I'll share my bat and I'll share my ball,
I'll share my books although you're small...
but *please* don't ask for my pirate ship;
that is just for me.

Judith Nicholls

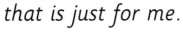

Early years wishing well: Toys and games

Sharing with Ali

Personal, social and emotional development

★ Talk to the children about how much more fun they can have with their toys if they share them with their friends, brothers and sisters. How do they feel when somebody invites them to share their toys?

★ Invite the children to talk about their favourite toy and why it is special to them.

★ Set up activities where the children are encouraged to share materials and be on hand to reward positive behaviour.

Communication, language and literacy

★ Talk to the children about times when they share. Encourage them to write or draw about these times on large 'speech bubble' shapes which could then be suspended from your ceiling.

★ Rather than each child choosing their own book at quiet reading time, encourage the children to choose a book with a friend. One child may choose to read to the other or the children can look at the illustrations together.

Mathematical development

★ Ask a small group of children to estimate how many beads there are in the bead box. After they have counted the beads challenge the children to divide the beads into equal shares for each group member. Allow the children time to work out their own strategies before you intervene.

★ Introduce the children to balance scales as a method of sharing items evenly.

★ Use a collection of same-sized plastic bottles in the water tray to encourage the children to find out about sharing and capacity.

Knowledge and understanding of the world

★ Make a Victoria sponge cake, explaining to the children that the mixture has to be shared between the two tins and then sandwiched together. Share the cake at snack time.

★ Let the children colour and cut their own paper birthday cake on the photocopiable sheet on page 88. Ask them to decide how many friends will share the cake, and how will they fold and cut the cake to make sure that they all have an equal share.

Physical development

★ Invite the children to play games with a partner such as 'Row, row, row the boat' and throwing and catching to encourage sharing.

Creative development

★ Set up a play tent as a place where children can go with a friend to share some quiet talking time or to read a book together. The tent could be made into an igloo, a secret cave or a hot-air balloon.

★ Ask the children to choose a friend to paint a picture with. This will entail the children sharing both equipment and decision making.

Early years wishing well: Toys and games

Everol's statue

'Gather round,' said Mr Clarke, 'I'm going to teach you a new game.'

The children in Mr Clarke's class sat down on the dry grass and listened.

'It's called Statues, and...'

'I've played that before,' said Mandy.

'I don't want to play,' said Everol. 'When it was my birthday, I didn't win Pass the parcel or Musical chairs. I didn't win *anything*.'

'Never mind, Everol,' said Mr Clarke. 'Here's how we play Statues. I stand with my back to you and you go and stand side by side in a line over there. Then you creep up and touch me on the shoulder.'

'That's too easy,' whispered George.

'BUT,' said Mr Clarke, 'I can turn round suddenly and if I see you creeping, you're out. As soon as you see me turn round, pretend you're a statue and stand very still. If I see you moving, or hear you making a sound – you're out.'

'What's it got to be a statue of?' Everol asked.

'Can it be an animal?' asked Jessie. 'Like that big lion in the park?'

'It can be a statue of anything you like,' said Mr Clarke.

The children stood in a line and Mr Clarke turned his back.

'Start!' he shouted. The children crept forward. Suddenly, Mr Clarke looked round and all the children froze...

Except Mandy, who was pretending to be an ostrich.

'You wobbled, Mandy,' said Mr Clarke. 'Go and stand by the tree!'

Mr Clarke turned his back again and the children crept forward. Suddenly, Mr Clarke looked round and all the children froze...

Except Nathan who was pretending to be a hippo.

'I can see you giggling, Nathan!' said Mr Clarke. 'Go and stand by the tree!'

Mr Clarke turned his back again and the children crept forward. Suddenly, Mr Clarke looked round and all the children froze...

Except Stuart who was pretending to be an aeroplane.

'I can see you waving about, Stuart!' said Mr Clarke. 'Go and stand by the tree!'

Mr Clarke turned his back again and suddenly Everol touched him on the shoulder!

'Well done, Everol!' said Mr Clarke. 'You've won! You take my place now and we start again. You were really quiet and still. What were you pretending to be?'

'I was a statue of my pet snail,' said Everol, proudly.

Geraldine Taylor

Everol's statue

Personal, social and emotional development

★ Play some party games with the children that involve winning and losing. Encourage the children to understand that enjoying taking part in the games is as important as who wins.

★ Tell the children the fable of 'The Hare and the Tortoise' from *Aesop's Fables* (Puffin) and discuss the moral of the tale.

Communication, language and literacy

★ Make a collection of descriptive phrases such as 'as still as a statue' and 'as flat as a pancake'. Challenge the children to make up some phrases of their own with the same structure 'as … as a …'.

★ Create an 'Our pets' book, asking the children to make contributions of drawings, writing or photographs. Try to arrange for a local vet to come to talk to the children about how to care for their pets.

Mathematical development

★ Use a sand timer to find out what can be done in a minute! Find out how many times the children can count to ten, or run up and down the play area before the time runs out and they have to stop.

★ Play 'Statues' and as each child is caught out, count the children who are in or out. Show the children how to use an abacus to do this.

Knowledge and understanding of the world

★ Show the children a collection of small articles that have moving parts such as a toy action figure and a clothes peg. Immerse each object into a separate plastic container filled with water and let the children place the containers into the ice compartment of a refrigerator. The next day show the children how the objects are trapped in the ice and are unable to move, just like the statues in the story.

★ Look at snails in the garden. Explain to the children that snails are very slow because they only have one foot, and they often leave a trail to let us know where they have been!

Physical development

★ Extend the game of statues by letting the children suggest different types of statues such as soldier statues, clown statues or ballerina statues.

★ Let the children play balancing games – with no wobbling!

Creative development

★ Visit a local statue or monument close to your setting so that the children gain a real understanding of what being 'as still as a statue' really means. Try to find out who made the statue and when it was erected. On your return to your setting, encourage the children to design their own statues from junk or construction equipment.

Toyshop teddies

On the way to school on Monday morning, Mum and I passed the toyshop. Five teddy bears sat in a row looking at us from the toyshop window.

One was brown like rich, dark chocolate.
One was gold like honeycomb.
One was black like the sky at midnight.
One was cream like buttermilk.
One was as white as new snow.

'Oh, please, may I have one?' I asked.

'Not now,' said Mum as we hurried past. 'We'll see tomorrow.'

On Tuesday morning when we passed the toyshop, four teddy bears sat in a row looking at us from the toyshop window.

One was brown like rich, dark chocolate.
One was gold like honeycomb.
One was black like the sky at midnight.
One was as white as new snow.

'Please, please, may I have one?' I asked.

'Not now,' said Mum as we hurried past. 'We'll see tomorrow.'

On Wednesday morning when we passed the toyshop, three teddy bears sat in a row looking at us from the toyshop window.

One was brown like rich, dark chocolate.
One was gold like honeycomb.
One was as white as new snow.

'Please, please, *please* may I have one?' I asked.

'Not now,' said Mum as we hurried past. 'We'll see tomorrow.'

On Thursday morning when we passed the toyshop, two teddy bears sat on the shelf looking at us from the toyshop window.

One was brown like rich, dark chocolate.
One was gold like honeycomb.

'Please may I have the brown one?' I asked. 'He's my favourite.'

'If he's there tomorrow,' said Mum, looking at the teddy bears as we hurried past.

On Friday morning we ran to the toyshop. One teddy bear sat on the shelf looking out at me. His fur was the colour of rich, dark chocolate.

'Look, Mum!' I said, but Mum didn't answer.

As I watched, the shopkeeper took the teddy bear out of the window. Someone had bought him! 'Oh, no!' I hid my face in my hands.

'What's wrong?' asked Mum after a while.

'We were too late,' I said.

'Oh,' said Mum. 'Have I bought the wrong one then?'

I took my hands away from my eyes. Mum held out a bag... and there inside was the teddy bear with the fur as brown as rich, dark chocolate!

Susan Quinn

Early years wishing well: Toys and games

Toyshop teddies

Personal, social and emotional development

★ It is sometimes difficult for children to understand that you have to wait for some things. Encourage the children to talk about any times that they found waiting difficult, such as for birthdays, Christmas or visits.

★ Ask each child to bring in their favourite bear to the setting and at circle time, ask them to talk about why their bear is special.

Communication, language and literacy

★ Play a circle memory game starting by saying 'I went to the toyshop and I bought a red teddy'. The child sitting next to you should repeat your sentence, then add a purchase of their own. Continue around the circle.

★ Talk about thank-you letters and ask the children to write and illustrate a thank-you letter after a birthday or special occasion.

Mathematical development

★ Make a collection of five bears to match the bears in the story. As you tell the story take away the bears as they are mentioned and each time count to see how many are left. Keep the bears available for the children to practise subtraction activities.

★ Number each of the five bears in your collection by pinning on a numbered birthday badge to encourage number recognition and ordering activities.

Knowledge and understanding of the world

★ Make a photographic record of a typical week in your setting. Display this with caption with the days of the week, 'Movement day is Wednesday'.

★ Make a collection of information books to find out about real bears. Where do they live and what do they eat?

Physical development

★ Copy the photocopiable sheet on page 89 onto different coloured paper. Encourage the children to join the dots, then carefully cut their bears out and decorate them. Use the cut-out bears to form a colourful border for a display.

★ Sing traditional teddy action rhymes such as 'Round and Round the Garden' and 'Teddy Bear, Teddy Bear Turn Around'.

★ Make a skittle game with your teddy collection. Sit five teddies in a line and show the children how to roll a ball (or toss a beanbag) from behind a line approximately two metres away from the teddies. Challenge the children to see how many they can knock over at one time.

Creative development

★ Cut out card teddies for a 'Toyshop teddies' display. Use a variety of textured materials for collage and attach the arms and legs with split pins so that the teddies can really move.

Fishing

'I'm sorry, Paul,' said Grandpa. 'We won't be able to go fishing today. Maybe the weather will be better tomorrow.'

Paul was very disappointed. He loved to sail out in the bay in Grandpa's little fishing boat, to fish for mackerel. But for days the weather had been too bad.

'Tell you what,' said Grandpa, 'we'll go fishing anyway, here indoors!'

Paul looked puzzled. 'How can we do that?' he asked.

'Well,' said Grandpa, mysteriously, 'we'll need card, paper, glue, scissors, coloured pencils, paper clips, two lengths of string and... two magnets!' It took them some time to find everything.

'Now, let's get to work,' said Grandpa. 'You take the paper and coloured pencils, Paul, and draw me some nice big fish.'

Paul drew some fish on the paper and gave them bright stripes and spots. Grandpa helped him to stick them onto the card. While the glue was drying, Grandpa asked Paul to draw an underwater scene on a long piece of stiff paper. Paul drew the sandy seabed with rocks, shells and seaweed. Then he put in some more fish, crabs and an octopus.

'That's lovely,' said Grandpa.

Grandpa glued one end of the picture to the other, to make a circle with the picture inside it.

'It looks like a round sea!' laughed Paul.

'Time to cut out the fish,' said Grandpa. They carefully cut round the fish that Paul had drawn earlier.

Then Grandpa tied one of the magnets to a piece of string. He tied the other end of the string to a pencil. Then he did the same with the other magnet.

'Fishing rods!' he said. 'Now we need to put paper clips on each of your fish. The magnet will stick to the paper clip and that's how we'll catch them!'

They put the fish into the round sea.

Then Grandpa and Paul 'fished' until lunchtime. Grandpa caught four fish and Paul caught six in the first game. But Grandpa beat Paul in the second game.

They were half-way through the third game when Gran called, 'Lunchtime!'

'What is it?' asked Paul. 'I'm starving!'

'Fish and chips,' said Gran, with a smile.

'As long as it's not fish and *paper clips*!' said Paul, and they all laughed.

Mandy Poots

Early years wishing well: Toys and games

Fishing

Personal, social and emotional development

★ Talk about the special things the children do when they visit their grandparents. If some of the children do not have grandparents invite them to talk about another special person that they visit.

★ How do the children feel when something special that they have been looking forward to is cancelled? Ask the children to share their experiences with the group.

Communication, language and literacy

★ This story includes instructions on how to make a fishing game. As you read the story, make a pictorial list which the children can use as a sequencing activity. Follow the instructions to make the game.

★ Make a collection of fiction and non-fiction books about fish and fishing and learn some fishy songs and rhymes.

Mathematical development

★ Let the children play with the fishing game that you have made. Give them a timer and ask them to find out how many fish they can catch in one minute. Make a tally of how many fish each child collects and announce the winning fisherman or woman at the end.

★ Start with five fish in the pool and as the children take one out, ask them to say how many are left. As the children become more able, add more fish to increase the challenge.

Knowledge and understanding of the world

★ Fill a clear, high-sided, plastic container or bottle with water. Drop some magnetic marbles and paper clips into the water and watch them sink to the bottom. Invite the children to retrieve the magnetic objects by using a horseshoe magnet on the outside of the container.

Physical development

★ Cut out and number some paper fish and place them on a parachute. Let the children make them leap and fly by flapping the parachute. Which fish will jump off of the parachute first? Which one last?

★ Give each child a copy of the photocopiable sheet on page 90. Ask the children to join the dots to complete the shapes on the fish and to colour it in using coloured felt-tipped pens or pencils.

Creative development

★ Make salt dough with the children and let them model their own small fish. Make a hole in each fish before you bake them in the oven. Invite the children to paint the fish in bright colours, then when they are dry, hang them from the ceiling in your setting.

★ Buy a fresh fish from the fishmonger's or supermarket. Encourage the children to draw the fish from observation, then show them how to use a piece of sponge and paint to fill in the shape.

Amy's first kite

Amy's family loved to fly kites. Every weekend they went out with the Kite Club. Amy was too young to join in, but she loved to watch the kites floating about in the sky: all different shapes, sizes and colours. Some looked like animals or faces.

But today was special. It was Amy's birthday. She was going to have a kite of her own at last, and they were going to Windrush Hill to fly it!

'No opening it until we are up on the hill,' said her mum, giving her the parcel.

Once they were on top of the hill, Amy quickly ripped off the wrapping paper. She was so excited.

The kite was just the right size. It was bright blue, with a seagull in the middle and a long white tail streaming from it.

'Right,' said her mum. 'Let's see how it flies, Amy.'

Amy couldn't wait to have a go.

First, her mum straightened out the two strings which were tied to the kite frame and wound them round the middle of the wooden holder so that they were not too long.

'Put one hand on each side of the string,' she said. 'I'll walk away and hold the kite up high. When I let go, you pull. Ready? Go!'

Amy pulled. The kite twirled round... and went crashing into the ground.

'Try again, Amy,' laughed her dad. 'Pull gently.'

This time the kite zoomed up. But it swooshed away and went crashing into a bush.

The next time it landed on top of a hedge.

Amy was disappointed. 'It's too hard,' she said. 'I'll never do it.'

'You will,' said her mum. Amy tried once more. She pulled more gently. This time her kite flew straight up into the sky until it seemed as if the seagull was really flying. Soon she felt brave enough to try curving it this way and that. Amy laughed out loud as she watched the long tail sailing after it.

'That's it! You've got it!' said Mum.

'At this rate, it won't be long before you're ready for a stunt kite!' said Dad.

Amy was thrilled. She felt the tug of the wind on her hands as her first, blue kite soared high in the sky, and she knew that this was going to be a special day for her to remember for ever.

Patricia Leighton

Amy's first kite

Personal, social and emotional development

★ Can the children recall what it is like waiting for their birthdays, and the excitement when the day actually arrives? Encourage the children to talk about their own birthday experiences.

★ Introduce the children to a range of other festivals, celebrated by different faiths, where gifts are given.

Communication, language and literacy

★ Let the children play outside on a windy day, then ask them to describe how the wind makes them feel. Help them to devise short sentences about their experience and make these into a group 'Wind' poem.

★ Make a kite alphabet by giving each child a kite shape to paint in their favourite colours. Stick a different letter of the alphabet onto each kite and display them in alphabetical order.

Mathematical development

★ Copy the photocopiable sheet on page 91 for the children and ask them to carefully cut the kites out. Encourage the children to order the kites for size.

★ Cut out a collection of paper triangles and ask the children to tessellate them to make kite shapes. When the children are satisfied with their kites, encourage them to stick the shapes onto a sky-coloured piece of paper.

Knowledge and understanding of the world

★ Look at a real kite and let the children discover how it is made, and from what materials. Cut some nylon kite fabric into streamers for the children to fly on a windy day. Hang some of the streamers from a tree outside so that the children can gain some understanding of wind power and direction.

★ Talk about things other than kites that move in the wind such as hot air balloons, flags and the leaves on trees.

Physical development

★ Go outside on a windy day and let the children move and be blown by the wind. Take some bubble mixture and wands outside with you and let the children enjoy blowing bubbles in the wind.

★ After the children have been doing physical exercise ask them to put their hands on their chests. Can they feel their hearts beating? Talk about why we should exercise regularly.

Creative development

★ Look at books about Chinese kites. Make a kite display with a theme in your setting. Encourage the children to pose questions about the different kites and display the questions with the kites.

★ Make some kite-shaped print blocks with the children and challenge them to make some wrapping paper with a repeat pattern.

The weather house

Sara had been given a weather house for her birthday. She stood it on her dressing table. The little house had a thatched roof, four windows and two doors. On days when it was going to be sunny weather, a lady wearing a flowery dress and a sun-hat came out of one door. On days when it was going to be rainy, a man in a raincoat, holding an umbrella, came out of the other door. Sara looked at her house every morning to see if it was going to rain.

'Good morning, Mrs Sunshine,' Sara said to the weather lady on the first day of her holidays. 'I'm very glad to see you our of your door today because I am going to play with my friend Lucy in the garden.'

Sara and Lucy had fun in the garden. They played horses with the skipping ropes round their tummies as reins. They took turns to be the horse. Then they played with Sara's mini golf game.

'I'll come and play again tomorrow,' said Lucy.

But next morning the rain man had come out of his door.

'Oh, no. It's you, Mr Rain,' said Sara to the weatherman. 'You can't come out today because I want to play in the garden with Lucy!'

She pushed the rain man back into the house, stuffing paper tissues into his doorway so that he could not come out again.

But it rained anyway. It rained on Lucy when she ran up the road to play in Sara's garden.

'You can't make it stop raining,' said Sara's mum. 'And it's a good job, because the flowers would die without water. You and Lucy can still have fun indoors.' She pulled the tissues out of the rain man's doorway so he could come out again.

Sara and Lucy painted pictures, played with Sara's train set and then put on a concert for Sara's mum, playing a toy drum and recorder.

'I'm glad it rained today,' said Sara, when it was time for Lucy to go home. 'We had a really good time.'

'Can I come again?' said Lucy.

Barbara Ball

The weather house

Personal social and emotional development

★ Talk together about special friends and what makes them special. Encourage the children to think about how we make friends, what we need to do to keep our friends and how to help children who do not seem to have any friends.

★ Are there times that the children can remember when they were disappointed? How does it feel and what can we do to overcome these feelings?

Communication, language and literacy

★ Help the children to make two scrapbooks one called 'Things to do on a rainy day' and another 'Things to do on a sunny day'. Invite the children to find or draw pictures to stick into the books and keep them in the reading corner with a collection of other books about the weather.

★ Make a collection of wet weather and sunny day songs such as 'I Hear Thunder' and 'Incy, Wincy Spider'.

Mathematical development

★ Make a weather chart using the weather symbols on the photocopiable sheet on page 92. Keep a tally of how many dry and wet days there are in a whole month.

★ Set up a mini golf course in your play area using skittles and tunnels. Give the children small soft balls and long cardboard tubes to use as clubs and encourage them to count how many strokes they take to get their balls around the course.

Knowledge and understanding of the world

★ Place some blotting paper into two plastic trays and sprinkle on some cress seeds. Water one tray but not the other and encourage the children to see what happens and recognize that all plants need water to live.

★ Keep some pine cones or seaweed in the setting and watch what happens to them as the weather changes.

Physical development

★ During outdoor play, chalk large rain, sun and wind weather symbols around the play area. At the blow of a whistle, shout either 'It's raining', 'It's sunny' or 'It's windy'. The children should run to the correct symbol and mime either putting up umbrellas, lying down to sunbathe or flying a kite.

Creative development

★ Make two doorways into your role-play area. Decorate one half of the area both inside and out with a sun, blue sky and beautiful flowers and give the children sun-hats and sun-glasses to wear. On the other half of the area, display grey clouds, pictures of rain and puddles and in this area, let the children wear rain hats and wellington boots for splashing in puddles.

The toyshop

Mum had to go shopping but Laura and Oliver had colds, so Uncle Peter came to look after them.

'It's not fair. I want to go shopping, too!' moaned Laura.

'So do I,' grumbled Oliver. 'It's boring at home!'

'Cheer up,' said Uncle Peter. 'How about if we play at shops, instead?'

'Can we play at *toyshops*?' asked Oliver.

'Of course,' said Uncle Peter. 'Come on, let's go and fetch your toys.'

Uncle Peter carried down the box of toys from their bedroom. Laura and Oliver brought the till and play money. Uncle Peter helped Laura and Oliver write different prices on small pieces of paper and stick them onto the toys.

'Right, Oliver can be the shopkeeper first,' said Uncle Peter. 'You and I can be the customers, Laura.' He shared out some play money.

Oliver stood behind the table, pretending it was the shop counter. He felt very important.

Laura looked over the toys. 'I'd like that teddy bear, please,' she said, pointing to a yellow teddy bear. The price ticket said thirty pence. Laura counted out the coins and gave them to Oliver.

'Thank you,' said Oliver. 'Have you seen our special offer this week?'

Laura shook her head.

'If you buy two of these farm animals, you get another one free!' said Oliver, pointing to their wooden Ark animals.

'Um...,' Laura looked at her money. The farm animals were ten pence each. She only had fifteen pence left.

'Here, I think you dropped this,' said Uncle Peter, handing her a five pence piece.

'Oh, thank you,' said Laura. Now she had enough. 'I'd like an elephant and a giraffe... and... a zebra, please.'

She gave Oliver twenty pence. Then it was Uncle Peter's turn.

'Have you got something for a boy about six?' Uncle Peter asked Oliver.

Oliver looked at all the toys left on the table. 'I think these roller boots would be just right,' he said, grinning. They were, of course, his own roller boots.

They all took turns to be customers and shopkeepers and had a lovely time. They were so busy playing that they did not hear Mum come home.

'I'm back!' called Mum. 'What a day!' she sighed. 'The shops were crowded, it started to rain and the bus was late. It's a good job you two didn't come with me.'

Laura and Oliver were glad, too. Shopping at home was much more fun.

Karen King

Early years wishing well: Toys and games

The toyshop

Personal, social and emotional development

★ Talk about how we feel when we are are not well and ask the children what makes them feel better.

★ Discuss the idea of different toys being suitable for different ages. Compare the children's favourite toys now with toys that they might have had when they were babies.

Communication, language and literacy

★ Encourage the children to write shopping lists for different events and read *The Shopping Basket* by John Burningham (Red Fox) at story time.

★ Make a collection of phrases used in shops such as 'Buy one, get one free' and 'Shall I help you pack your bags?'. Display these as signs in a shop role-play area.

Mathematical development

★ Make a collection of small toys and price them initially at 1p each. Give each child a purse with five 1p coins in for them to gain understanding of paying and receiving. Extend this activity with larger prices or more coins as the children gain confidence.

★ Set up some empty shop shelves using large construction blocks. Lay out a collection of items for sorting and ask the children to sort and place the collection on the shelves. Ask the children to explain their sorting criteria to you.

Knowledge and understanding of the world

★ Arrange a small group visit to a local greengrocer. Ask the children to write a list of fruit needed for that day's snack and give them purses and bags to carry. If the greengrocer is willing encourage him or her to talk to the children about selling fruit and vegetables and about where in the world some of the fruits are grown.

★ Some children will have experience of currencies other than pounds sterling. Encourage the children to bring this currency into the setting and make it a starting point for discussion about other countries, customs and holidays.

Physical development

★ Play simple team games which involve the children taking turns to run and exchange a beanbag for a quoit from 'the shopkeeper' and running back to join your team.

★ Encourage the children to play games with a friend such as throwing and catching, or taking turns with bats and balls.

Creative development

★ Set up a shop in the role-play area, it could be a toyshop like the one in the story or a shoe shop, a pet shop or a grocery shop depending on your current topic.

★ Use coins with paper and wax crayons to make rubbings and with play dough to make prints of faces and the edge patterns.

Our computers at school

I love our computers! In class we have to take turns to have a go or we would all be playing on them all the time! We can write stories or do number games or put things in the right order.

Sometimes I work with my friend and we have a competition to see who gets most things right. The computer even adds up the score for us at the end so we can see who's won the game.

There's a little arrow on the computer screen called the cursor. You move the cursor with the mouse! It's not a real mouse but it does have a sort of long tail that joins it to the computer. It goes 'click' whenever you press one of the sides, left or right. You point the cursor at the numbers or letters or pictures and go 'click' on

the answer. If you get the answer wrong, or lose a point in the game, the computer makes a funny ringing noise.

My favourite game is 'The circus'. There are people and animals that do tricks and play games as you point and click on them. You can choose their clothes and hats and even the tricks that they do. You have to be quick or the computer chooses them instead.

There's a place free at one of the computers now. I'm going to choose 'The circus' game and dress up the clowns with curly hair and baggy trousers. If I'm quick enough I might be able to put them into their little cars and watch them race around!

Stevie Anne Wilde

Our computers at school

Personal, social and emotional development

★ Talk to the children about the importance of taking turns. Introduce a tick list system for turns on the computer, or other activities. The children will soon understand that by using this system, they will have a fair turn at activities.

★ Talk about winning and losing. Ask the children if it matters who wins as long as everybody is joining in and enjoying themselves.

Communication, language and literacy

★ Use a suitable font on the computer to make a name card for all of the children. Ask each child to write their own names, using the name cards as a reference.

★ Consider using a paint program on the computer and ask the children to use the pencil to write their names freehand, this will develop good mouse control.

Mathematical development

★ Use a floor robot to challenge both programming and numeracy skills. Introduce calculators to the children and with practise they will be able to tally and total numbers with ease.

★ Make the children aware of the way that numbers are constructed on calculator displays. Challenge the children to make similar number shapes using spent matches.

Knowledge and understanding of the world

★ Tell the children that the computer is not the only programmable machine in their lives. Most children will also have knowledge of appliances such as washing machines and microwave ovens. Ask them to find out what programmable machines are in their homes.

★ Some children may have programmable toys that they could bring in and show to the group, under supervision.

★ Ensure that you are aware of any children entering your setting who have a computer at home. Some children have considerable ICT understanding and need to be challenged with suitable programs.

Physical development

★ Cut out some large arrow shapes and set up an adventure play trail outside for the children to follow, or a route on a play road map to follow with the toy cars.

★ Make a set of cards carrying instructions such as 'Three steps forward' and 'Jump up and down on the spot'. During a movement time shuffle the cards and call out one instruction at a time for the children to follow.

Creative development

★ Challenge the children to draw their own pictures using a painting program on the computer. As their skills increase, provide an increased range of options and encourage them to print out their own work.

Grandpa's toys

One day, Grandpa fetched a really big box down from the loft. It was full of toys that he had when he was little. Inside was a train set. It had an engine, a tender and trucks, some straight lengths of rail and curved ones. Grandpa showed me how the rails slotted together to make a track in the shape of a number eight. I tried to see how the engine worked, but then Grandpa told me it was a clockwork train. He wound the engine with a tiny key and put it on the rails. He pressed a lever and off it went, rattling along the lines and pulling the trucks behind it.

Then Grandpa showed me a toy steam engine that really worked. He put some special purple liquid in a pot and lit the wick, then he filled a tin box above the wick with water. The tiny flame heated the water and made it steam. After a while, the steam made the engine work. Wheels turned and cogs clicked round. It was amazing. Grandpa told me that the steam engine was his favourite toy when he was a boy.

I looked to see what else was in the box. I found cars and lorries and a red London bus. They were made of metal and the paint was chipped in places. Grandpa called them his Dinky toys. The word Dinky was stamped in the metal under each one, to show who made them.

Then Grandpa took out his farm animals. Some were made of hard plastic but most were metal. Grandpa picked up a toy sheep. He told me that it was the oldest animal of the lot. It had belonged to his mother – my *great* grandma – and was made of a very early sort of plastic, called celluloid. If it got anywhere near a fire it would burst into flames, so he put it back in the box. Toys today are much safer.

There was one last thing in the box. It was a teddy bear. It only had one eye and was losing its stuffing. There was something hard and round inside it. Grandpa explained that when the teddy bear was new, it had made a growling noise when you pressed its tummy. It didn't work any more but, sometimes, it's good to keep things even when they are old.

Celia Warren

Early years wishing well: Toys and games

Grandpa's toys

Personal, social and emotional development

★ The concept of a keepsake will be quite new to most children. Invite an older person in to explain to the children why it is important to keep some things, even if they are worn out or broken. Ask if they could show the children a keepsake of their own and explain its importance to them.

★ Pose questions such as 'Are new toys always the best?'. Invite the children to talk about their favourite toys and why they are so special.

Communication, language and literacy

★ Go on a pretend journey in a role-play train. Think about where you are going, who you are going to visit and what you will see on the way.

★ Make some tickets for your role-play train journey and gather a collection of brochures and posters about rail transport.

Mathematical development

★ Challenge the children to make a 'figure of eight' track with the train track. Use eight trains, eight people, eight trees and eight animals to encourage counting.

★ Find a box and count in five toys. As you take each toy out of the box, encourage the children to work out how many toys remain in the box to encourage early mental numeracy skills.

Knowledge and understanding of the world

★ Ask a grandparent or great-grandparent to visit the setting to talk to the children about the toys that they had and the games that they played when they were children. Local resource libraries often have collections of old toys that can be loaned to illustrate talks.

Physical development

★ Sing action rhymes such as 'Down by the Station, Early in the Morning' and 'Teddy Bear, Teddy Bear, Touch Your Nose' in *This Little Puffin*… compiled by Elizabeth Matterson (Puffin).

★ Show the children a selection of wind-up toys and explain how they work. Encourage the children to mime being wound up, let loose and slowing down and stopping. Suggest that they could be trains, engines or animals.

Creative development

★ Help the children to create some instruments using junk materials and objects from around the setting. Encourage the children to use the instruments to accompany themselves when singing a new version of 'The Wheels on the Bus' from *This Little Puffin...* with verses such as 'The rattling train goes…' and 'The growling bear goes… .

★ Listen to the 'Dance of the Toys' from the ballet *Coppelia* by Delibes. Can the children identify which toys are dancing to the music.

Grandma's doll's house

I love visiting Grandma. She has lots of interesting things. My favourite is a big doll's house which is very old. Although I can't play with it, Grandma lets me look inside.

There are six rooms in Grandma's doll's house and two hallways.

Downstairs is the kitchen and dining room.

The kitchen has an old-fashioned stove that lights up as if it's really working. Tiny apples and oranges are in a bowl on the table and copper pots and pans hang on the wall near the stove. There's a doll dressed as a cook with a wooden spoon in her hand.

The dining room is across the hall. It has a large table and four chairs. On the table are tiny plates the size of my thumbnail and tiny silver knives and forks. In the corner, a doll wearing an old-fashioned dress is playing the piano.

Upstairs is the living room that Grandma says was called the parlour in those days. It has a white fireplace and a fire with coals that glow red. Around the walls are bookcases filled with different-coloured books and there's a grandfather clock in one corner that really tells the time.

At Christmas time, Grandma puts a holly wreath on the front door of the doll's house and a Christmas tree in the parlour. I love to see the fairy lights on the tree twinkling through the doll's house window.

Across from the parlour is the bedroom. It has a wardrobe, chest of drawers and a big, high bed. A small table with a tiny candle in an old-fashioned holder stands next to the bed.

Grandma has to lift up the roof so I can see the attic rooms on the top floor.

My favourite room is the nursery. This was where the children would spend most of their time. It's filled with all sorts of toys: trains, blackboard, dolls and teddies. My favourite of all is a grey-spotted rocking horse with bright red reins. Next door to the nursery is a tiny room for the maid.

When I asked Grandma where the bathroom was, she told me that in those days most houses didn't have bathrooms. Before she told me that, I used to wish I could live in Grandma's doll's house!

Susan Quinn

Grandma's doll's house

Personal, social and emotional development

★ Convert the role-play area into a different room in the house each week. Start with the kitchen, then the living room, bedroom and bathroom. Involve the children in discussions, decision-making and co-operative play and let them help with the removals and the decorating!

★ Explain to the children that most people have something that is very precious to them, which may not necessarily be valuable, that we must respect if we are asked not to touch it. Ask the children if they have any precious belongings.

Communication, language and literacy

★ Explain any new vocabulary in the story that the children may not understand such as what a maid is, what old-fashioned means and what is special about a grandfather clock.

★ Sing some of the less familiar nursery rhymes such as 'Ride a Cock-horse' and 'Diddle, Diddle, Dumpling'.

Mathematical development

★ In the role-play house, challenge the children to lay the table for a certain number of guests. Encourage them to count the cutlery and crockery and to work out how many sandwiches and cakes will be needed for tea.

★ Use the nursery rhyme 'Hickory Dickory Dock' and the grandfather clock mentioned in the story, as a stimulus to talk about watches, clocks, timers and the passing of time.

Knowledge and understanding of the world

★ Go for a walk in your locality and look for different types of homes. Talk to the children about their own homes and how different their lives would be like if they lived in a castle, an igloo or on a boat.

★ Challenge the children to find out why it is traditional to bring holly into the house and put coins in the pudding at Christmas time.

Physical development

★ During dance and movement time pretend to visit different rooms in the doll's house. Ask the children to pretend to mop the floor, chop the wood and polish the silver. Can the children decide which are fast and which are slow movements?

★ Act out some favourite nursery rhymes and choose children to be Humpty Dumpty and the King's men. Let the children be Jack and Jill and go tumbling down the hill!

Creative development

★ Make a group doll's house using shoeboxes and found materials. Help the children to develop one room at a time and combine ideas from the story, alongside the children's own knowledge about the contents of their own homes.

Dressing up

At nursery, I love to dress up with my friend, Sadia. We go into the dressing-up corner and decide what to wear. There are some uniforms, especially small to fit boys and girls. A uniform is what people wear to show what job they do such as a nurse, crossing patrol person and train driver. One day, Sadia and I pretended that two dolls had been to hospital to have their tonsils out. Sadia put on the doctor's white coat and listened to the dolls' chests with a stethoscope. I wore the nurse uniform and took the dolls' temperatures with my thermometer. We gave our patients jelly and ice-cream to eat – only pretend! Sadia has had her tonsils out, so she knows that you get jelly and ice-cream to eat.

There are lovely hats to wear. Sometimes we play weddings, like when my auntie married her boyfriend. My favourite hat for weddings is the pink straw one with the flowers around the brim, but Sadia likes the blue and white striped one with the little net veil to hang over her face. She likes peeping through it.

The ordinary clothes, not uniforms, hang on a rail and the big red box is full of belts, bags, scarves and gloves.

Today Nathan plays with us as well. We are dressing up to go to a ball, like Cinderella in the story that Miss James told us. We all put on sparkly dresses, so long that they reach the floor. We'll have to hitch them up when we walk so that we don't trip over. Nathan helps fasten my buttons. I help Sadia with her zip.

Shereen drives past on the dumper truck, wearing a hard hat and bright orange waistcoat. She's a builder delivering bricks to her friends over there that are building a wall.

Now we want shoes. There are about ten different pairs on the shelf. The three of us put on strappy high heels. We help each other stand up. It's not easy! We practise walking. We wobble and giggle a lot. Some beads now, and we're ready for the ball.

At tidy-up time, we put everything away in its right place. Nathan says that we could make a train tomorrow with a line of chairs and all be train drivers. That's a good idea, so perhaps we'll do that.

Susan Eames

Dressing up

Personal, social and emotional development

★ Ask the children what they would like to be when they grow up and why. Invite visitors into the setting to tell the children about their jobs, the clothes or uniforms that they have to wear and their special responsibilities.

★ Invite a member of the local clergy into your setting to talk about weddings. Consider having a role-play wedding in your setting where everyone can dress up and the children can invite guests and help to prepare a reception.

Communication, language and literacy

★ Encourage the children to paint pictures of themselves doing the jobs that they want to do when they grow up. As they are working, record what they say about their chosen jobs and display these comments alongside their paintings.

Mathematical development

★ Make a collection of different shoes for the children to sort into pairs. Talk about other pieces of clothing that come in pairs such as socks and gloves. Can any of the children count in twos?

★ Sort the dressing-up clothes into outfits with clothing, a belt, a bag and shoes for each person. Encourage the children to use one-to-one correspondence to count out what they will need.

Knowledge and understanding of the world

★ Invite a local health carer (perhaps a parent) into the setting to explain to the children the importance of healthy eating.

★ Ask the children to think of other people who help us in our daily lives such as the crossing patrol person and the refuse collectors and encourage them to find out more about these jobs. Introduce appropriate costumes into the dressing-up box.

Physical development

★ During movement time, retell the story of Cinderella. Let all of the children be Cinderella as she sweeps the floor, collects what she needs to go to the ball, dances with the prince and tries on the glass slipper.

★ When the children are dressing or undressing, encourage them to help each other. Positive encouragement will help the children to achieve and they will enjoy their new-found independence.

Creative development

★ Help the children to make a train with the chairs. Allow each child to take a ticket before boarding the train and choose a train driver and a ticket collector.

★ Encourage the children to make some decorations to enhance some of the hats in your setting such as adding paper flowers to decorate a wedding hat or jewels to decorate a crown.

A musical box

On the shelf in my uncle's room next to his books, there is a small house made of wood. Uncle Tony lets me pick it up but I have to be extra careful because it's very precious. The outside looks like a house, but inside it's just an empty box.

Now I will tell you a surprise. When you lift up the roof on the house, it plays a tune. It's a musical-box house! When the roof is up you hear music, but when the roof is down, the music stops. At first, I thought it was magic, but Uncle Tony pulled up the floor inside the house to show me how it works. Underneath the floor, there are some little pieces of machinery that make the music. There are no batteries inside. It's all done by clockwork and there is a key sticking out underneath to wind up the machinery. If the music starts to go slower or stop, Uncle Tony turns the key round and that makes the music go at the right speed again.

I have listened to the tune so many times that I can sing along with it now. Sometimes I dance as well.

Uncle Tony says that the correct name for the house is a *chalet (shal-lay)*.

The chalet has six widows and two doors – one at the front and one at the back. I like the balconies outside the bedroom windows. The logs in a pile next to the front door look just like the real logs that some people burn in their fireplace. The roof has two sloping sides that go up to a point and there's one chimney.

My uncle told me the true story about how he got the musical box. When he was six, his dad went on holiday to a country called Switzerland. There are high mountains in Switzerland and lots of snow. Some people live in chalets built mostly of wood. The musical-box house looks just like one of those chalets. Uncle's Tony's dad bought the musical box in a shop and brought it all the way back home to give to his little boy. That little boy grew up and he's my Uncle Tony. That's why he has the musical box on his shelf.

I'm very pleased that Uncle Tony looked after his musical box. He thinks it's beautiful and so do I.

Susan Eames

A musical box

Personal, social and emotional development

★ Have a table or shelf where children can safely place their own special things that they bring in from home. Set aside time to let the children talk to their friends about their special things and to say why they are special to them.

★ Encourage the children to recognize that people are precious as well as possessions.

Communication, language and literacy

★ Show the children a collection of postcards. Give each child a blank postcard and ask them to draw pictures on the front of the postcards and write their messages on the back. Provide some postage stamps for the children to stick on their cards before they post them in the role-play post-box.

★ Work on a simple family tree with the children to help them to understand what grandparents, uncles, aunts and cousins are. Remain sensitive to individual family circumstances.

Mathematical development

★ Go on a walk in your locality to count windows on houses, make a tally of the door colours or look at the shapes of roofs.

★ Make a collection of sturdy plastic boxes and allow the children to work with them in the sand or water trays to discover more about capacity.

Knowledge and understanding of the world

★ Invite the children to look at information books about different types of homes. Talk together about what it would be like to live in a home that is very different from our own.

★ Make a collection of toys and clocks that have clockwork movements. Find an old broken clock that you can open up and encourage the children to use a magnifying glass to take a closer look at the springs and cogs that make a clock work.

Physical development

★ Make a large cardboard key and during movement time, explain to the children that you are going to wind some of them up. Tell them that they will have a minute to dance (timed with a large sand timer) and when they stop they will have the opportunity to watch the next group of dancers.

Creative development

★ Use two finger puppets and explain to the children that one of the puppets likes fast singing and the other likes slow singing. Start singing at an ordinary pace and when one of the puppets comes from behind your back the children will have to speed up or slow down their singing pace.

★ Find a box large enough to hold a tape recorder and decorate it like a house. Each time the 'musical box' is opened play the children some music from different countries.

Party games

(Tune: 'Merrily We Roll Along')

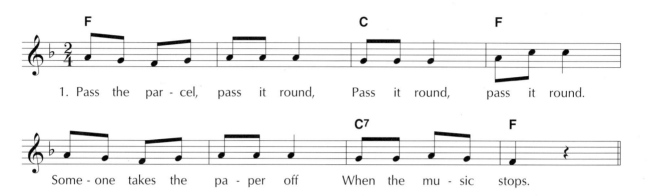

1. Pass the par-cel, pass it round, Pass it round, pass it round.

Some-one takes the pa-per off When the mu-sic stops.

2. Wave your arms, and dance about,
Dance about, dance about.
Then you sit down on the floor
When the music stops.

3. Walk around the empty chairs,
Empty chairs, empty chairs.
Then you sit down on a chair
When the music stops.

4. Close your eyes, and find someone,
Find someone, find someone.
Can you guess the person's name?
Then you have a look.

5. Put the tail on Donkey's back,
Donkey's back, Donkey's back.
Put the tail on Donkey's back
Then you have a look.

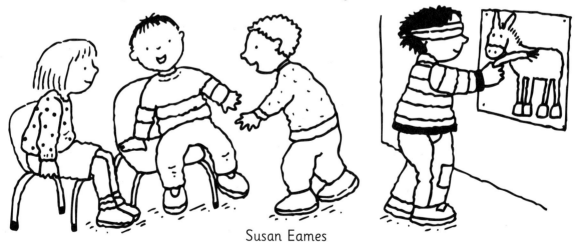

Susan Eames

Early years wishing well: Toys and games

Party games

Personal, social and emotional development

★ Invite the children to identify the games mentioned in the song and to talk about their own experiences of parties. Introduce the party games to the children gradually, explaining that some games have winners, but not all of them.

★ When the children are familiar with the games, let them help to organize a party in the setting. Ask them how they can make sure that everybody enjoys the party.

Communication, language and literacy

★ Encourage the children to make lists of the games that they would like to play, the children and adults that they would invite and the food that they would like to eat at a party.

★ Challenge the children to design an invitation letter and to write their friends' names on the invitations.

Mathematical development

★ Make a party cake with a group of children, involving them in weighing ingredients, following instructions, cooking and decorating the cake. Another group of children could be responsible for cutting the cake into equal portions and serving the guests at the party. A further group could have the responsibility of counting the correct number of cups and for pouring the drinks.

★ Ask the children to make some paper chains, creating repeat patterns using two or three different-coloured papers.

Knowledge and understanding of the world

★ Find out about party games that children play in other parts of the world. Learn the rules and try to incorporate some of these into your own party programme.

★ Remember to explain the safety aspects of the party games to the children before they start to play, emphasizing taking turns, not rushing about and being aware of each other.

Physical development

★ Make up a counted sequence of movements with the children to include waving arms, jumping and turning. This will help the more self-conscious children to feel a little more comfortable with dancing games.

★ Ask the children to find a partner and to take turns in leading each other around some simple obstacles, with one of the children's eyes shut. This will help to increase the children's confidence in each other.

Creative development

★ On large sheets of thin paper, ask the children to paint or print to make wrapping paper. When the paper is dry, let the children practise wrapping up some toys.

★ Ask the children to paint a donkey to make their own 'Pin the tail on the donkey' game to take home and play.

Six little teddies

1.*Six lit - tle ted - dies on the shelf to - day. Six lit - tle ted - dies wait - ing
there to play. One lit - tle ted - dy jumps on the floor. How ma - ny ted - dies on the
shelf? *Pause to count:* Five lit - tle ted - dies on the shelf.

Five little teddies on the shelf today...
And so on.

*Or any number that you choose to start with.
Use real teddies to accompany the song.
Continue the verses until all the teddies have
jumped off; some may need a push!*

Susan Eames

Early years wishing well: Toys and games

Six little teddies

Personal, social and emotional development

★ Talk with the children about how they need to take care of each other when they are playing. Explain that they should tell an adult if they are unhappy or not feeling safe when they are playing outside.

Communication, language and literacy

★ Tape record the children singing the song and other number rhymes. Provide headphones for the children to play back the tapes and to enhance their listening skills.

★ Try 'hot seating' a bear. Let one child pretend to be one of the bears that has jumped from the shelf and invite the other children to ask questions about the bear's experience. Ask 'Were you injured when you fell from the shelf?' or 'Were you pushed?'.

Mathematical development

★ Sit the teddies along a number line (reading from the children's left to right) with a teddy corresponding to a number as you sing the song. The first teddy to jump is the one at the highest number, making it easier for the children to see how many are left.

★ Challenge the children to sort six teddies from the smallest to the biggest then add a number line. Discuss the meaning of 'bigger than', 'smaller than' and encourage the children to link the numbers with the sizes, saying, for example, 'bear number three is

bigger than bear number one'. When the children are familiar with the six bears, ask them to close their eyes and remove one bear from the line. Can they describe the bear that is missing when they open their eyes?

★ Draw six bear faces onto a strip of paper and number them. Encourage the children to use a dice and to cover the bear corresponding to the number thrown.

Knowledge and understanding of the world

★ Find out what the children know about real bears such as how many different kinds of bear there are, where they live and what they eat.

★ Set up a bear environment in the sand tray, with plenty of rocks and pebbles for the children to build caves for small-world bears.

Physical development

★ Set up some low apparatus, on which the children can practise balancing and then jumping. Remember to remind the children to bend their knees when they jump.

Creative development

★ Help the children to recreate the song in an interactive display. Make six large bears using different art techniques such as paint, collage and printing. Hang the bears from a line of numbered cup hooks and encourage the children to use them when singing the song together.

Let's play Tig

(Tune: 'Polly Put the Kettle On')

1. Let's play Tig when we go out. I'll be 'on,' you run a - bout.

If I catch you, you're on next. Let's all play Tig.

2. Let's play Hide-and-Seek outside.
Close your eyes, and we will hide.
Then you come and find us all. That's
Hide-and-Seek.

3. Mr Wolf, what time is it?
We creep forward bit by bit.
When you say it's dinnertime
We turn and run.

Susan Eames

Let's play Tig

Personal, social and emotional development

★ Talk about the things mentioned in the song that we do every day in houses. Ask the children to think of things that they do every day to look after themselves.

★ Using cut-up copies of the photocopiable sheet on page 84, encourage the children to work in small groups to build houses from the shapes.

Communication, language and literacy

★ Place an easel between two children. Ask one child to paint a picture of a house and describe what they are doing to the other child, who should follow the description and try to paint a copy.

★ Invite each child to share with the rest of the group what their own home is like by bringing in a photograph.

Mathematical development

★ Help the children to make a 'Maths house' book with information about each child's house on each page – perhaps the shapes of the windows, the number of doors and how many people live there, in size order.

★ Give each child their envelope of shapes (see Physical development) and a sheet of A3 paper. Use positional language and shape names to instruct the children to make matching house pictures, for example, 'Put the triangle above the large square'.

Knowledge and understanding of the world

★ Ask the children to make houses from boxes, cutting out windows and covering the holes with fabric or Cellophane. Place a torch into each house to light them up.

★ Select pictures from magazines or museum postcards showing how homes have changed through time. Focus on the size of houses, building materials and types of windows and roofs. Invite the children to find differences between the pictures and their own houses.

Physical development

★ Show the children how to make rubbings of brick walls. Invite them to cut these into house shapes and print features such as doors and windows using shaped sponges and paint.

★ Give each child a copy of the photocopiable sheet on page 84 and help them to cut out the shapes. Ask them to write their name on an envelope and place the shapes inside.

Creative development

★ Look at photographs of gardens and visit a real one. Provide a selection of materials and ask the children to create collages of gardens. Encourage them to include imaginative features such as ice-cream trees or football flowers.

★ Notice the views from windows in your setting and encourage the children to paint them. When the paintings are dry, mount them with cardboard windows over them that open to reveal the view.

Bath toys

I've got a boat to float in the bath, It tick-les my toes and makes me laugh.

My rub-ber duck goes quack, quack, quack. You push it to the bot-tom and it bobs right back.

David Moses

Early years wishing well: **Toys and games**

Bath toys

Personal, social and emotional development

★ Encourage the children to talk about why we have baths or showers and wash our bodies and hair. Tell them that to keep healthy we need to look after our personal hygiene.

★ Explain to the children that different things make us laugh. Write a list of all of the things that the children say make them laugh. Leave the list of things that make them sad for another day!

Communication, language and literacy

★ Read the story of *Five Little Ducks* by Ian Beck (Orchard Books) and 'read' the pictures with the children as well as the text.

★ Use small-world farm animals to encourage conversation between the children. Talk about the noises that the different animals make.

Mathematical development

★ Make a collection of plastic bottles for the children to play with in the water tray. Encourage them to use terms such as 'float', 'sink', 'empty' and 'full'.

★ Create five card boats with the children and number them from one to five. Shuffle the boats and give one each to five children to hold up in front of the group. Challenge the rest of the children to put the boats in the correct order.

Knowledge and understanding of the world

★ Collect a variety of objects from around your setting and ask the children to discover what happens to these objects when they are put into the water tray. Can the children say why some objects float and some sink?

★ Make a collection of different materials such as wood, rubber and plastic and talk together about how they feel and what we use them for.

Physical development

★ Take the children outside and explain to them that one area of the playground is for things that float and one for things that sink. When you call 'boat', the children should run to the floating area and when you call 'brick', they should run to the sinking area and so on. When the children are clear about the rules, let them take over the game.

Creative development

★ Introduce the children to the technique of marbling. Use blue and green inks to make a marbled background, then encourage them to paint, or cut and stick, pictures of their favourite bath toys on top.

★ Play some gentle music such as *A Day Without Rain* by Enya (EMI) and ask the children to close their eyes and listen to the music. Talk about how the music makes them feel and play the music again while the children paint or draw their reactions to it.

Jigsaw bits!

(Tune: 'Hot Cross Buns')

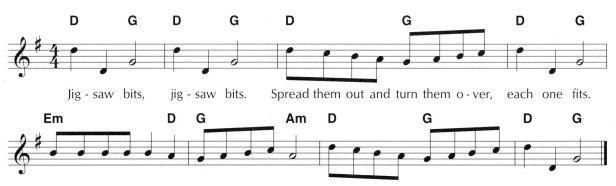

Jig - saw bits, jig - saw bits. Spread them out and turn them o - ver, each one fits.

Cor - ners put out rea - dy, ed - ges near - ly done, Puz - zle pie - ces, puz - zle pie - ces, jig - saw fun!

Sue Nicholls

Early years wishing well: **Toys and games**

Jigsaw bits!

Personal, social and emotional development

★ Make a list of jobs that the children can help with in the setting. Invite them to talk about the jobs which they enjoy doing and to say why. Suggest that everybody should help in some way, especially at tidying up time.

Communication, language and literacy

★ Choose a favourite story and read the first few pages to the children. Stop reading and offer the children two options for what might happen next. Challenge the children to say why they make their choices. Encourage them to listen carefully and to use their recall skills to make the correct choice in order for the story to continue.

Mathematical development

★ Hold up a square piece of card, fold it in half diagonally and talk to the children about the different properties of squares and triangles. Cut the card into four and ask the children to reassemble the square. Allow the children to design their own jigsaws by using the photocopiable sheet on page 93, drawing a picture, cutting out the pieces and then fitting it back together

★ Have a look at some of the jigsaw-puzzle boxes that you have in your setting and point out that there is a number on the boxes. Count the puzzle pieces together to check that the numbers correspond. If the children make their own puzzles, encourage them to write the correct number of puzzle pieces on the front of their boxes.

★ Use sorting boxes to encourage the children to talk about the properties of three-dimensional shapes including the words corners, edges and faces.

Knowledge and understanding of the world

★ Make a collection of toys and other resources that fit together such as a lock and key or a teapot and its lid. Invite the children to discover the different ways in which these resources fit together by screwing, locking and twisting.

Physical development

★ Place four different-coloured hoops in the corners of your outdoor play area. Divide the children into four teams and give each child an appropriately-coloured band. Ask the children to run about and say that when you shout 'Jigsaw' they should run to the correct coloured hoop and form a ring around it with their team-mates.

Creative development

★ Fold an A4 sheet of paper into eight equal spaces and open out. Make potato print blocks and challenge the children to make a print to fit into each of the eight spaces. Encourage the children to see similarities between their patterns and wrapping paper.

Rocking horse

Rock - ing horse goes to and fro, Climb on the sad - dle and off you go.

Ride your horse and hold the rein And gal - lop a - way and home a - gain.

Sue Nicholls

Early years wishing well: Toys and games

Rocking horse

Personal, social and emotional development

★ Ask the children to tell you about a visit that they may have made to a farm or a zoo. Encourage them to talk about the animals that they saw and how they were cared for.

★ Talk together about caring for pets and other animals in our environment.

Communication, language and literacy

★ Encourage the children to think of other words to replace the word 'away' in the song. Perhaps the horse could be galloping to town or to the shops!

★ Ask the children to clap the rhythm of the song as they sing it. Challenge them to individually clap the syllables of their own names.

★ Encourage the children to help you make pictorial lists of words to describe how different animals move such as horses gallop, snakes slither and kangaroos jump.

★ Play a game of 'I spy' starting with 'I-spy with my little eye something beginning with 'h' galloping down the street'.

Mathematical development

★ Use the small-world animals to develop the children's counting skills. Ask the children 'If one horse has four legs, how many legs would two horses have altogether?' or 'If one chicken has two legs, how many legs would three chickens have altogether?'.

Knowledge and understanding of the world

★ Invite a local person who rides a horse to come and talk to the children and to bring in some of the equipment needed to look after their horse such as a saddle, reins, blanket and brushes.

★ Find out about the shoes that horses wear and compare their footprints to those of other animals.

Physical development

★ Set up a route in the outdoor play area for the children to follow on the wheeled vehicles. Ask them to go fast or slow, forwards or backwards and encourage the children to greet each other as they pass by.

★ Let the children experience the 'rocking' beat of the music by sitting crossed-legged opposite a partner and holding hands (to represent holding the reins) and 'see-sawing' to and fro. in time to the rhythm of the song.

Creative development

★ Give each child a copy of the photocopiable sheet on page 94 copied onto card. Invite them to colour and decorate the two rocking horses, then to cut them out and join them together using the tabs.

★ Ask the children to select instruments that reflect the sounds of different animals such as coconut shells to make the sound of a galloping horse and a rainmaker to sound like a slithery snake.

Red balloon

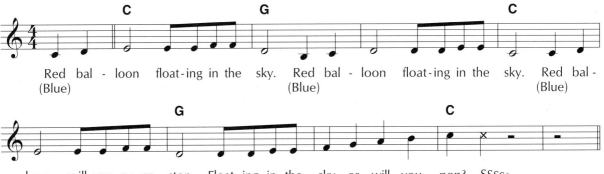

Red bal - loon float-ing in the sky. Red bal - loon float-ing in the sky. Red bal -
(Blue)   (Blue)   (Blue)

- loon will you ev - er stop Float-ing in the sky or will you pop? SSSSSSSS

Clive Barnwell

Early years wishing well: Toys and games

Red balloon

Personal, social and emotional development

★ Cut out a large hot-air balloon shape from a stiff piece of card and ask the children to decorate it with stripes of their favourite colour. Hang a small basket from the balloon and suspend it from the ceiling.

★ Explain to the children that the balloon will only fly if the basket is not too heavy. How will they decide who should go for a balloon ride and who should stay? If they were travelling alone in the balloon, what they would take with them and what would they leave behind?

Communication, language and literacy

★ Read the children the story of *The Blue Balloon* by Mick Inkpen (Hodder and Stoughton) and relate the events in the story to those in the song of the 'Red balloon'.

★ Inflate and tie a balloon for each child. Do not allow the children to blow up the balloons themselves or to play with deflated balloons. Secure a luggage label to each balloon with the child's name and the address of the setting. Take the balloons outside and let each child watch their balloon fly away. Explain to the children that if somebody finds their balloon they might get a letter to let them know how far their balloon travelled.

Mathematical development

★ Sing songs such as 'The Grand old Duke of York' and the 'Hokey Cokey' to develop awareness of positional language.

Knowledge and understanding of the world

★ Make a collection of different pumps such as a balloon pump, water pump, bicycle pump and bellows and invite the children to discover how they work. Encourage the children to use tubes and straws in the water to find out more about air.

★ Can the children think of other toys that need air to make them work such as space hoppers and footballs?

Physical development

★ Show the children what happens when you blow up a balloon, indicating not only the effect on the balloon but on the person blowing it up. During movement time, encourage them to use this information, to mime blowing up a balloon and then pretend to be those balloons as they float away, slowly deflating or suddenly going pop!

Creative development

★ Inflate some balloons and encourage the children to smear them with petroleum jelly. Cover some with papier mâché and wind others with lengths of wool and string dipped in PVA glue. When the coatings have dried, pop the balloons underneath and remove them leaving the balloon shapes for the children to decorate.

Spinning on the end of a string

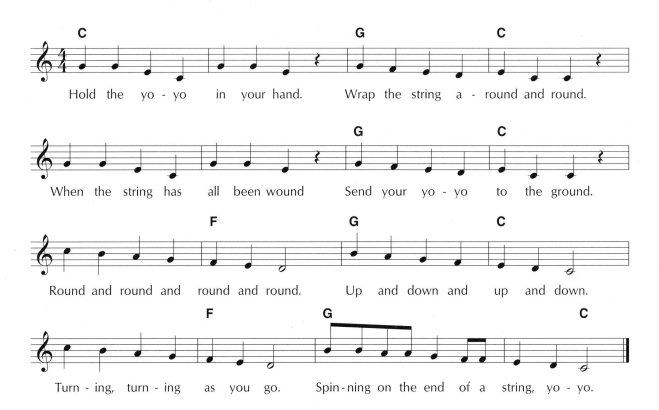

C   G   C

Hold the yo - yo in your hand.   Wrap the string a - round and round.

G   C

When the string has all been wound   Send your yo - yo to the ground.

F   G   C

Round and round and round and round.   Up and down and up and down.

F   G   C

Turn - ing, turn - ing as you go.   Spin - ning on the end of a string, yo - yo.

Clive Barnwell

Early years wishing well: Toys and games

Spinning on the end of a string

Personal, social and emotional development

★ Talk to the children about the fun that they have working and playing together, taking turns and enjoying themselves in your group.
★ Help the children to imagine how different it would be if everybody did not care for each other and play together.

Communication, language and literacy

★ Sing action songs with words, for example, 'in and out', 'up and down' and 'round and round' such as 'In and Out the Dusty Bluebells', 'Hickory Dickory Dock' and 'The Wheels on the Bus' from *This Little Puffin...* compiled by Elizabeth Matterson (Puffin).
★ Discuss the meanings of some of the more unusual movement phrases such as 'ups and downs', 'topsy-turvy' and 'in a spin'.

Mathematical development

★ Play with real yo-yos and encourage the children to notice as they wind them up how the string becomes shorter and shorter. Introduce the word 'spiral' and cut out some circles on which the children can draw their own spirals and cut them into springs.
★ Invite the children to sit in a circle and talk together about the shape that they have formed. Explain that many circular things roll such as yo-yos, hoops and wheels. Challenge the children to think of other circular things in the setting.

Knowledge and understanding of the world

★ Make a collection of other toys that also go up and down such as pogo sticks and jack-in-the-boxes. Ask the children to compare these with the movements of the yo-yo.
★ Challenge the children to use the construction toys to make playground equipment that goes up and down such as slides and see-saws.

Physical development

★ Invite the children to play with balls and to practise throwing and catching. Let them try bouncing and rolling balls to a partner.
★ Ask each child to stand in a hoop and to hold the hoop with both hands. Introduce the descriptive vocabulary from the song and ask them to make similar movements with their hoops. Explain that they must take account of the other children working close by, as well as feeling secure within their own space.

Creative development

★ Make a copy of the photocopiable sheet on page 95 on to card for each child. Provide felt-tipped pens for the children to colour the designs. Secure the completed yo-yos to a large piece of card using split pins and staple it to a display board. Invite the children to spin their designs and to talk about how the patterns and colours change. Add descriptive words as labels and make a collection of spinning toys to add to the display.

My little car is fun to push

(Tune: 'The Animals Went in Two by Two')

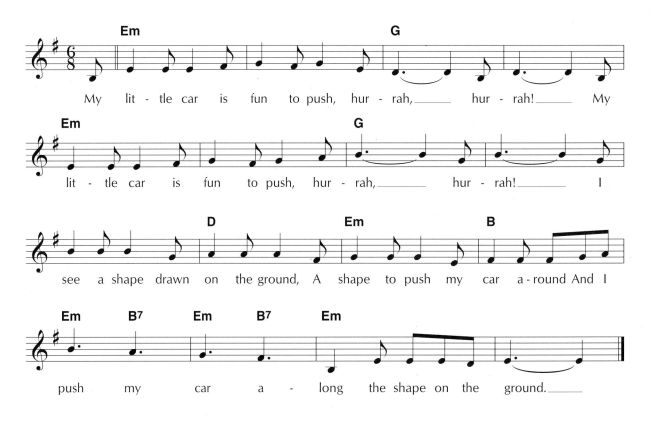

My lit-tle car is fun to push, hur-rah,_____ hur-rah!_____ My

lit-tle car is fun to push, hur-rah,_____ hur-rah!_____ I

see a shape drawn on the ground, A shape to push my car a-round And I

push my car a - long the shape on the ground._____

Sanchia Sewell

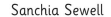

Early years wishing well: **Toys and games**

My little car is fun to push

Personal, social and emotional development

★ Give the children some safety mirrors to look into and talk about why we use mirrors in cars. Ask the children to tell you why they think that a driver looks into a mirror and how he or she knows when it is safe to overtake another vehicle.

Communication, language and literacy

★ Read the story *Mr Gumpy's Outing* by John Burningham (Puffin) to the children. Discuss the safety issues of taking so many passengers in one car and also the experience of working together to get something done.
★ Prepare some strips of paper with a road drawn along the bottom edge. Invite the children to draw their own home on the left-hand side of the strip and where they would like to go at the right-hand side. Encourage them to draw or write about what they might pass on the way from their home to their destination.

Mathematical development

★ Draw a big shape on the ground, or on a large sheet of strong paper, and encourage the children to follow the shape with their toy cars, while you sing the song together.
★ Draw a different shape such as a square, circle or triangle on the ground and, this time when singing the song, replace the word 'shape' with the name of the new shape.

Knowledge and understanding of the world

★ Invite the children to use their toy cars in individual shallow trays of wet sand. Encourage them to look at the marks they are making and to compare one set of tyre marks with another.
★ Challenge the children to make a wheeled vehicle using the construction equipment. How will they make their vehicles move? Discuss pushing and pulling and the option of making a slope. What difference does the gradient of the slope make to the distance covered by the vehicle?

Physical development

★ Collect some large cardboard boxes, big enough for a child to sit in, and invite a child to sit in the box. Encourage discussion on how the box and child could be moved. Think about vehicles with which the children are familiar such as sledges and trolleys.
★ Invite the children to talk about how they feel when they try to push or carry heavy things using all their energy. Can they feel their hearts thumping? Do they feel hot and sticky?

Creative development

★ Develop your role-play area into a car. Have a steering wheel, seats with belts, maps, a tool chest and a picnic basket and invite the children to act out the story of 'Mr Gumpy's Outing' together.

Early years wishing well: Toys and games

Beanbag song

(Tune: 'Row, Row, Row Your Boat)

C .... G

1. Take your bean - bag, put it on your head.

C .... G C

Shake your head a - round un - til the bag drops to the ground.

2. Take your beanbag, put it on your toes.
Lift the beanbag off your toes and put it on your nose.

3. Take your beanbag, put it on your chin.
Squeeze the beanbag with your hands and make it very thin.

4 Take your beanbag, hide it away.
Where is it, where has it gone?
You've found it hip-hooray!

Sanchia Sewell

Early years wishing well: Toys and games

Beanbag song

Personal, social and emotional development

★ Encourage the children to understand that regular exercise is as important as a healthy diet. Invite a health visitor in to the setting to talk to the children about healthy lifestyles.

Communication, language and literacy

★ Challenge the children to invent some new verses to the song that involve placing the beanbag on different parts of their bodies.

★ Recite the words but leave out the second rhyming word of each verse to encourage the children to listen carefully and to join in with a suitable response.

Mathematical development

★ Ask the children to sort some beanbags by colour, then ask them to sit around a spread-out parachute and to hold on tightly. Explain the game of 'Popcorn' which involves tossing three beanbags of each colour onto the stationary parachute, shouting the word 'Popcorn' and letting the children flap the parachute vigorously to try to make the beanbag 'popcorn' fly off! Stop occasionally to work out how many beanbags are left and how many have flown off.

Knowledge and understanding of the world

★ Talk to the children about healthy foods. Invite them to taste a selection of different beans such as baked beans, butter beans and runner beans. Let the children handle the beans before they are cooked and then see if the cooking process has altered their appearance. (Check for any food allergies or dietary requirements.)

★ Use the photocopiable sheet on page 96 to help the children learn the different body parts, inviting them to use a pencil to connect the words to the relevant part of the body. Draw around a child on a large piece of paper and invite one child at a time to toss a beanbag onto the body shape. The child must try to name the body part the beanbag touches and then the whole group can sing the appropriate verse of the song.

Physical development

★ Give each child a beanbag to practise their balancing skills while they sing the song.

★ Sing other action songs that involve body parts such as 'Head, Shoulders, Knees and Toes' in *This Little Puffin* … compiled by Elizabeth Matterson (Puffin).

Creative development

★ Make card collages with a collection of different dried beans and pasta. Give the finished collages a coat of PVA to secure it onto the card and to bring out the colours of the beans.

★ Fill old socks with dried beans and invite the children to make their own beanbag toy using scraps of fabric, buttons and wool.

Coloured glasses

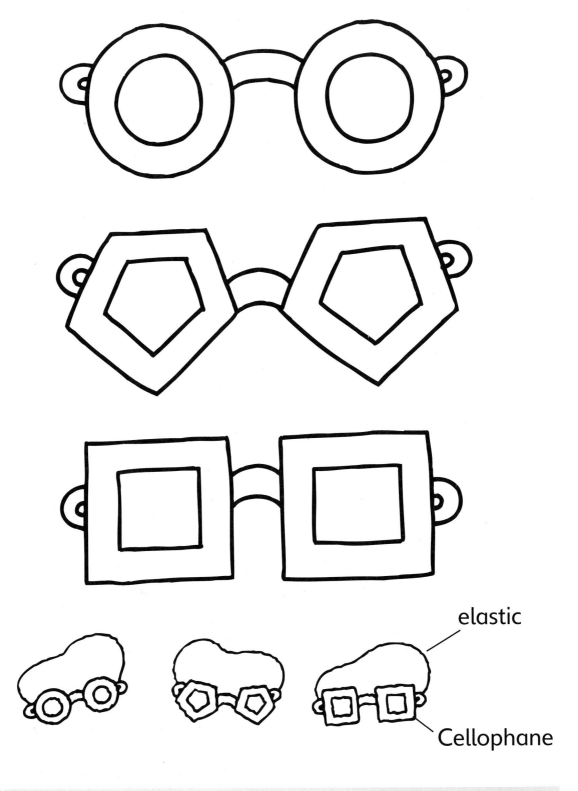

elastic

Cellophane

Different dinosaurs

Beautiful bubbles

Let's make a boat

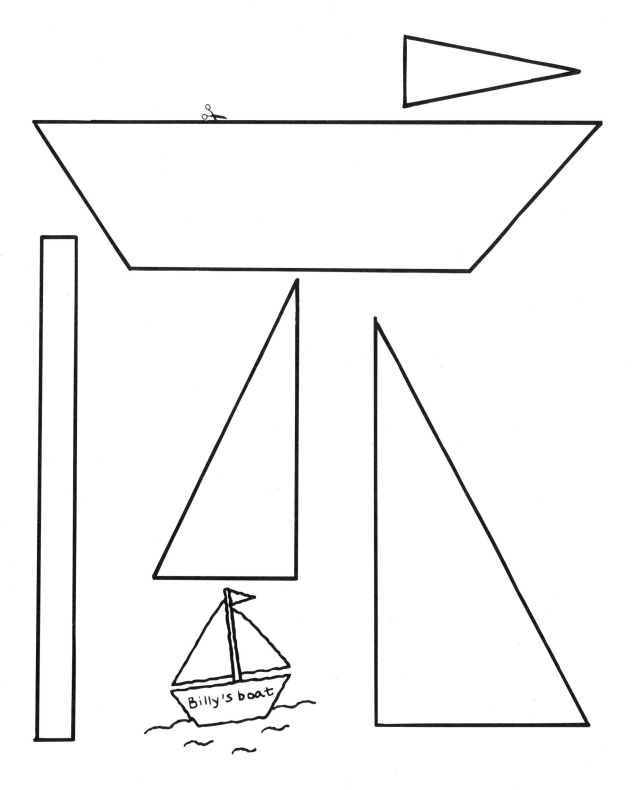

Billy's boat

Build a tower

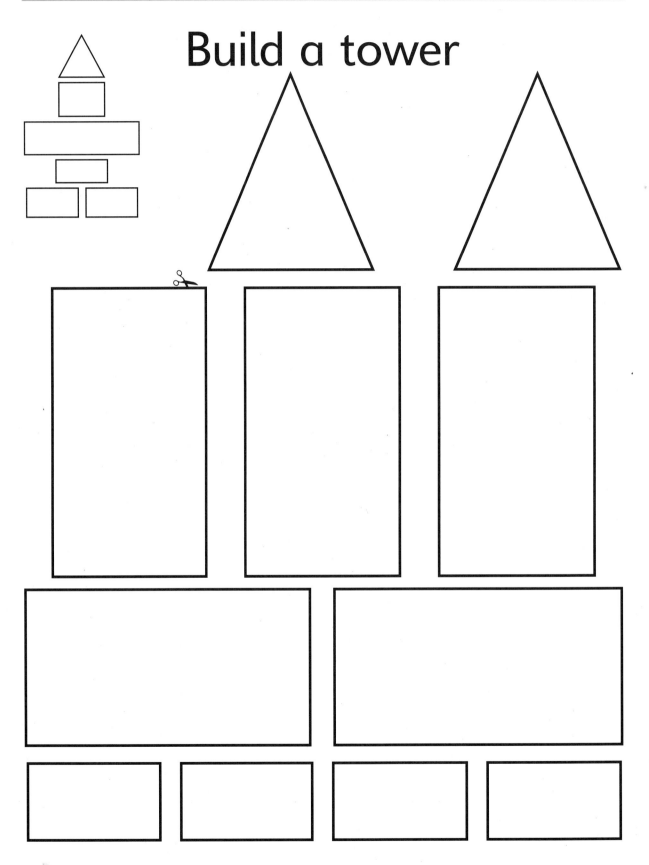

Design a robot

■SCHOLASTIC

Spiral snakes

Moving puppet

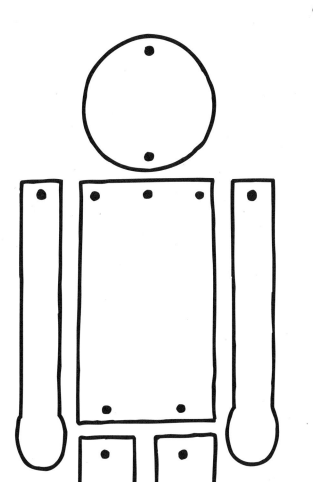

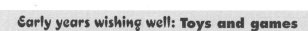

Birthday cake

How will you share your cake?

Teddy bear

Patterned fish

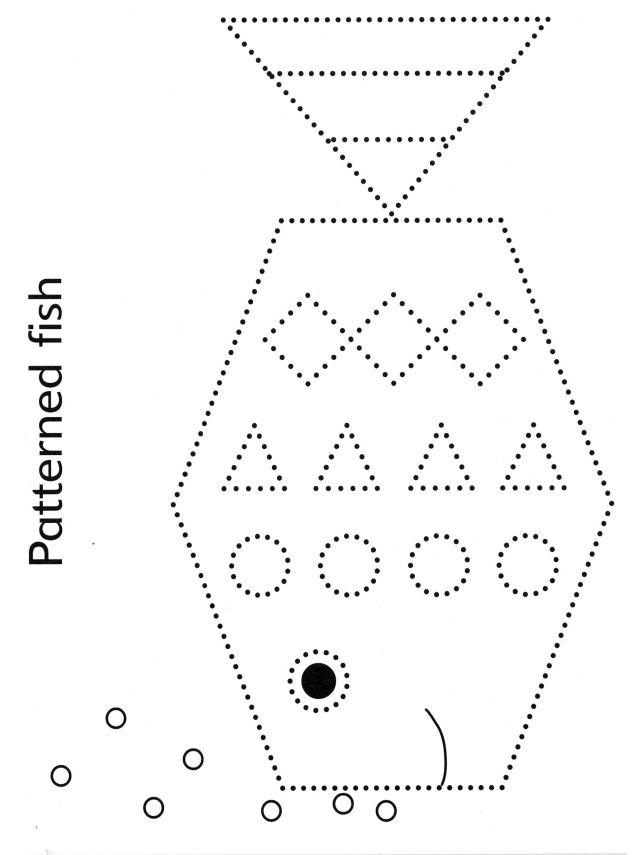

Colourful kites

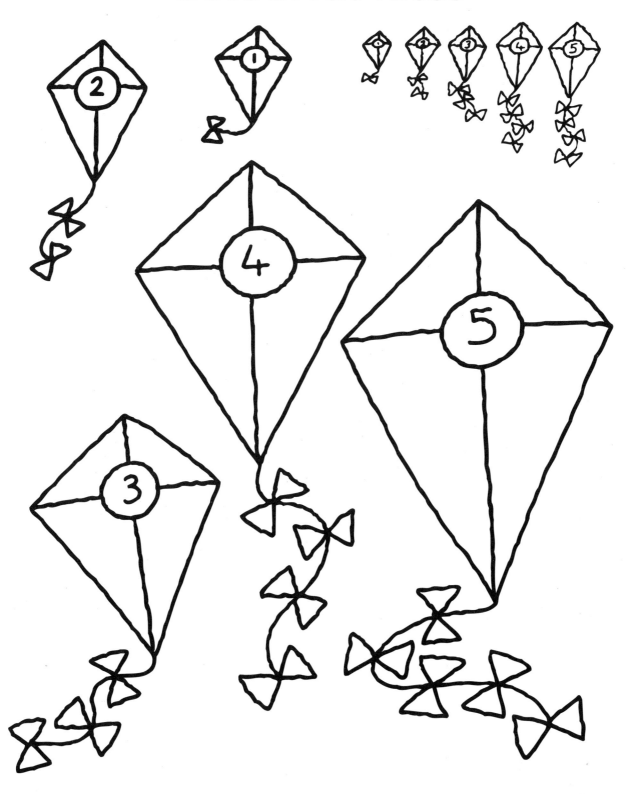

Weather symbols

Jigsaw puzzle

My rocking horse

Make a spinner

◀SCHOLASTIC

It's my body

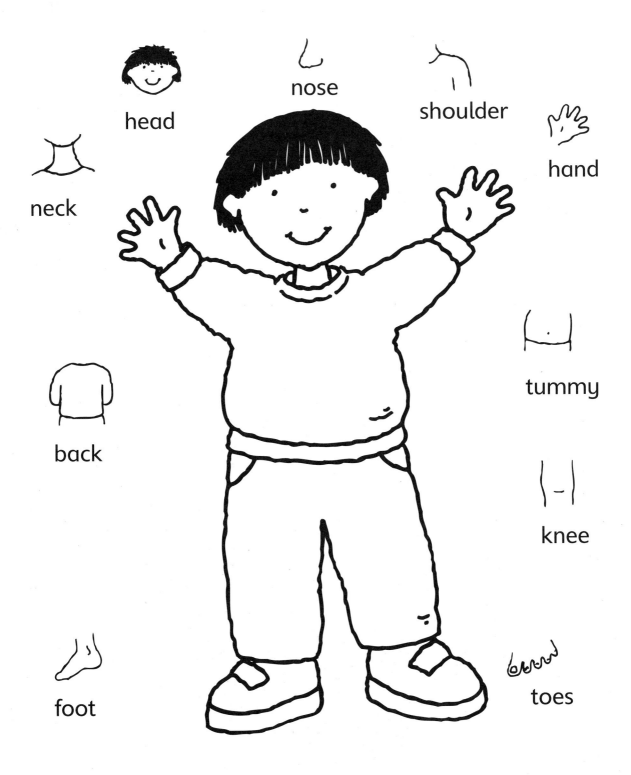

nose

head

shoulder

hand

neck

tummy

back

knee

foot

toes

SCHOLASTIC